A SPOONFUL OF COURAGE FOR THE
Sick *and* Suffering

"A Spoonful of Courage provides the remedy for those who don't feel well. Instead of "take two aspirins and call me in the morning," Dr. Page delivers dose after dose of courage in small *spoonfuls* that are easy to swallow."

— **Larry J. Leech II**, Author, Writing Coach and Cancer Survivor

"A much-needed Rx from our health care leadership."

— **Richard Harris**, MA Thm, Hospital Chaplain, Nacogdoches TX

"I have always believed in sharing relevant life experiences through story-telling. Dr Charles Page has not only been exposed to numerous examples of people in crisis but in his book, he has masterfully recounted their stories in a way that communicates powerful and practical life lessons. Those lessons are told within a clearly articulated Christian context and are reinforced by highly relevant scriptural references. Every one of the 45 stories in his book could be the subject of a meaningful and life-enriching discussion in a Bible study class or in a small discussion group session."

— **Fred Sievert,** Retired President of New York Life Insurance Company, Author of: *God Revealed* and G*race Revealed,* www.StoriesofGodsGrace.com.

"This book records the wisdom and spiritual insights of a Christian physician, as he shares some powerful stories of 'ordinary people who have acted in extraordinary ways. A collection of true memoirs, the author reflects his inspiring faith walk and medical career. I love how each chapter begins with a true story, and expresses a strong faith, grounded in the Word of God."

Karen Jordan, Author of *Words That Change Everything: Speaking Truth to Your Soul,* karenjordan.com

"I was excited to read *A Spoonful of Courage*. I found the collection of short stories inspirational and very relatable. Dr. Page does a fantastic job of encouraging readers by pointing out how God intersects in our lives—even when we are not looking for it."

— **Darren Dake**, D-ABMDI, CI, CCI,

Host of *Coroner Talk* podcast and Founder of

Death Investigation Training Academy

"Difficulty visits us all. But Dr. Charles Page gives us a dose of true hope in *A Spoonful of Courage*. Combining medical expertise, common-sense tips, motivational quotes, inspirational stories, with a heaping amount of healthy humor, Dr. Page provides exactly what we need to get through life with our hearts and smiles intact."

— **Anita Agers Brooks**, Inspirational Life Coach,

International Speaker, Award-Winning Author,

and Host of *Tending Your Dreams* Podcast

A
SPOONFUL
OF
COURAGE
FOR THE
Sick *and* Suffering

Transforming Your
Greatest Challenges
into Your Biggest
BLESSINGS

248
PAG

CHARLES W. PAGE, MD

NASHVILLE

NEW YORK • LONDON • MELBOURNE • VANCOUVER

A SPOONFUL OF COURAGE FOR THE Sick *and* Suffering
Transforming Your Greatest Challenges into Your Biggest BLESSINGS

© 2019 CHARLES W. PAGE, MD

Published in New York, New York, by Morgan James Publishing. Morgan James is a trademark of Morgan James, LLC. www.MorganJamesPublishing.com

This work is not intended to replace the advice of sound professional medical advice. Where individuals are identifiable, they have granted the author and the publisher the right to use their names, stories, and facts of their lives in all manners, including composite or altered representations. In all other cases, names, circumstances and descriptions and details have been altered to render the individuals unidentifiable.

ISBN 978-1-64279-247-8 paperback
ISBN 978-1-64279-248-5 eBook
Library of Congress Control Number: 2018910388

Cover Design by:
Rachel Lopez
www.r2cdesign.com

Interior Design by:
Bonnie Bushman
The Whole Caboodle Graphic Design

In an effort to support local communities, raise awareness and funds, Morgan James Publishing donates a percentage of all book sales for the life of each book to Habitat for Humanity Peninsula and Greater Williamsburg.

Get involved today! Visit
www.MorganJamesBuilds.com

To my wife, Joanna, my daily spoonful of courage,
and too the senior adults at Fredonia Hill;
thanks for listening to my stories.

TABLE OF CONTENTS

FOREWORD

If, and when you ever have the worst medical trauma of your life, whether you're staring at the ceiling of an emergency medical vehicle, or receiving bad news at your bedside, you want someone like Dr. Page delivering the message or meeting you while you are being wheeled into an emergency room on the gurney. Why? I'll explain.

Imagine life is good with a wife, two pre-school children and you're living your dream with an occupation you love. Then trauma strikes . . . excruciating pain . . . and a swift ride to the ER.

Physicians examine extreme swelling in an appendage, x-rays are taken, and then you see puzzled expressions on the physicians' faces. You have what?

"Hemophilia."

The doctors go on to say, "How do we treat you? Infusion of a blood product called "Factor VIII? Let's call the pharmacist."

Hours later, after the infusion and discharge, the trauma was over— or was it?

You see, in 1983, most of the manufactured blood products were infected with Hepatitis C and/or HIV. Three days after I experienced the event I just described, I was admitted to the hospital, literally dying from Hepatitis C contracted from a blood infusion. I faced yet another trauma.

There wasn't really any treatment, except fluids and rest. I was sent home to recover or die. Thankfully, I recovered, but it took over six months, with some lasting effects.

In 1986, a test to detect HIV was introduced. My clinic suggested I be tested since I may have been exposed through the transfusion. And guess what? I won the medical catastrophe lottery, testing positive for HIV, which often led to AIDS. Trauma again.

My wife and I were told to use protection with sexual intimacy (which we did) because HIV was transmitted via this mode. We were careful.

In 1987, my wife presented to her physician with bad pneumonia symptoms and was quickly hospitalized. The physicians diagnosed it a pneumocystis carinii pneumonia—AIDS induced pneumonia!

Do the math. Three years before my testing and our preventative counseling, the risk exposure was high. And guess what resulted? My wife won the medical catastrophe lottery, this time. Our family faced trauma again.

Only Bactrim and AZT could treat this, and AZT was only obtained by petitioning the FDA for use. It would take three weeks to obtain the treatment—too late for my beloved wife. Me, my pre-school children, family and friends stood by her graveside, only three weeks later. Trauma again.

So why would I want a physician like Dr. Page meeting me at the ER, the OR, or delivering bad news?

Because I did not have a physician like him during these times. I felt alone with the stigma of HIV. I wrestled guilt that I unknowingly transmitted a deadly disease to my wife. As I dealt with my own health issues, bereavement, and being a single parent raising two traumatized pre-school aged children, life felt hopeless.

In *A Spoonful of Courage*, you will see a display of understanding, compassion, concern, and resolve, blended with a strong faith in God. These stories are what I needed when I went through the traumas I experienced.

In this inspiring and encouraging book, Dr. Page personalizes the patient's situation, diagnoses and addresses the medical issue, looks for God's purposes and lessons in the situation, and helps people focus on hope and what really matters in life. His patient stories "hook" you, allowing you to look at the life lessons, relate them to Scripture, and then he encourages you to apply the learned lessons to your own life.

—Dana A. Kuhn, Ph.D.

Founder of Patient Services Inc.

A not for profit serving 36,000 patients annually

ABOUT DR. KUHN:

If you've ever received a blood transfusion *without* contracting HIV or Hepatitis, you can thank Dr. Dana Kuhn. He became infected with both viruses during the early days of the AIDS epidemic. He subsequently lost his health and his wife to AIDS.

Even more remarkable than his adversity is how Dana chose to respond. He became an instrument for change. Dana challenged the government, the blood transfusion industry and their policies, advocating stronger standards for screening of blood products. As a result of his efforts, blood transfusions are now safer in the United States.

Later Dana founded PSI, a nonprofit which provides medications for patients with rare diseases. Often these costly medications are not covered by insurance, leaving those suffering with these rare conditions little hope for treatment.

Dr. Kuhn models the principles found in this book. Despite his challenges, his life reminds us how we can respond positively in tough situations and how we can transform our struggles into something which benefits others.

Chapter 1

ALL IS NOT LOST

Courage to Find Hope in the Ashes

A burning cloud of soot rose into the air and then disappeared into the darkness. The smoke, reflecting the lights off the fire trucks, changed back and forth, from red to black to blue. I gazed at the shuffling colors and hugged my children, watching years of work and a lifetime of memories burn. While the flames rose, my heart sank.

Firefighters emerged from the front door, scurrying like ants coming out of the ground. They gathered in the front yard, caught their breath and wiped black sweat from their brows, congratulating each other on a job well done. Success. No one had been injured.

A freakish power surge had set my medical building ablaze. In the wreckage, a truckload of *whys* filled my mind. *Why* did this happen? *Why* now? *Why* me? *Why,* God?

My wife squeezed my hand. "Honey, things could have been worse. All is not lost."

When the smoke cleared, I surveyed the damage with the fire marshal. Black water dripped from the ceiling. Soggy insulation covered the floor, squishing under my feet. Melted computers and stained cabinets were charred beyond recognition. As we walked through the devastation, I thought of the Bible passage encouraging us to build our lives on things of value. Scripture promised that fires would come. Wood, and hay—the stuff of earth—would burn. Only things built on the eternal would remain. I wandered through the rooms, examining the devastation. What remained? What endured that could help me rebuild my life?

I thought of the narrow staircase leading to an upstairs office, where I had often met with God. There, in that stairwell, this prayer-challenged doctor learned to pray. By climbing up the stairs on my knees, I learned to stay focused. When my mind wandered, I'd crawl up another step, drawing my distracted brain back to the task at hand.

Walking through the destruction, I realized I would miss my meeting place with God the most. My anticipation grew as we neared the staircase. Had it endured the fire?

I turned the corner and held my breath. When I looked up the dark, smoky stairs, I sighed in relief. The stairwell survived. I made my way up the steps, inspecting my hide-out. In that stairwell, I found things of eternal value that I could rebuild my life on: an old doctor's bag, a Bible, pictures of my children, and a burned cross on a charred wall. When I saw those articles, I realized I'd been given a unique opportunity. In midstream, I had another chance to remake my life stronger better than before.

The Doctor's Bag

My black doctor's bag rested at the foot of the stairs—a cherished gift received upon my graduation from medical school. A relic of days gone by, it served as a personal reminder of how medicine had been practiced for generations. Only recently, I'd started using it to carry my tools on visits to the nursing home. I had set it on the stairwell before leaving that evening.

Astonished, I realized the smoke gave the worn-out bag a shiny black polish. Black soot covered the old bag and made it look new again. An encouraging thought crossed my mind. *Although I don't have an office, I still have a practice. All is not lost.*

Though my practice would never be the same, I saw new meaning in that old bag. It wasn't the only thing that gave me hope.

The Bible

A Bible sat on the stairwell steps, its blue cover now blackened. That afternoon, prior to the catastrophe, I had knelt to pray with that Bible in my hands. I wiped off the soot and opened the cover. The contents endured. The words were still written in black and red. Not a page had been singed.

Clutching the Bible in my hands, I reflected on the situation and on its deeper meaning. Life's fires don't change eternal truths. God's purposes, principles, and promises remain. These are the truths we can hold on to during adversity. His purposes never fail. His promises always endure. Those unchanging principles can guide us through the flames.

Pictures on the Wall

Several steps higher, burned pictures hung on the wall. My wife had placed photos of our five children there. With an old rag, I gently brushed the soot from the portraits of my kids. I remembered the day we decked them out in western garb for their pictures—the memory made me smile. Like the bag, the images had a fresh look. The heat faded the color in the photos, giving them a grey, Ansel Adams appearance. I stared at the pictures and marveled.

I thought about my children and other people God had placed in my life, those who most needed my influence and encouragement. When everything else burns, our investments in others will remain. People are eternal. If we are wise, we will pour our energy, focus and time into them.

The Cross

At the top of the staircase, a cross hung on a wall. The once attractive piece, now singed by the fire, lay fastened over the charred wood behind. Discouraged and trying to hold back tears, I removed the disfigured cross. What I saw sent a chill through my bones. Behind it, the wall's stained beauty had been preserved. A beautiful imprint of the cross remained, surrounded by the blackened wall.

The stamp on the wall reminded me of a truth about suffering. The blaze may burn God's children, but it will never consume them. God never wastes our pain. Instead, if we let Him, God leaves His image behind. Like my burned wall, a wounded soul, although blackened by flames, will display the image of Christ even greater than before.

When our lives go through the fire of adversity, we should remind ourselves of the things that remain. If we're breathing, we still have a purpose. God has given us a new opportunity to show His love, adequacy, and power in our lives.

The Real Champions

Though difficult, my experience doesn't compare with tragedies endured by other people I have met. Nor does my resolve equal their courage. One of my patients battled end-stage lung cancer. Against all odds, fighting pneumonia, she lived nine months longer than anticipated. She wanted to see the birth of her first grandchild.

Another man watched his bedridden wife burn in a house fire. He tried but couldn't get her out before the flames consumed his home.

Somehow, despite the pain, he picked up the broken pieces, rebuilt his life and kept going.

I have seen everyday people respond in extraordinary ways, being their best in the worst of times. Their difficulties make them better, not bitter. They suffer well. Their lives reveal a depth of character, determination of spirit, and passion for life that defies human explanation. When I think of them, hope flourishes. I see the cross burned into their lives through their suffering. They are not famous, but they are faithful—everyday, ordinary people who have acted in extraordinary ways. These are their stories.

> *"Therefore, we do not lose heart. Though outwardly we are wasting away, yet inwardly we are being renewed day by day. For our light and momentary troubles are achieving for us an eternal glory that far outweighs them all. So, we fix our eyes not on what is seen, but on what is unseen, since what it seen is temporary, but what is unseen is eternal."* [1]

Chapter 2

THE DIY RANCHER

Courage to Come to the Great Physician

There was an old Texas rancher who loved home remedies. He had no use for doctors and medicines.

One chilly morning, the old man felt under the weather. His wife encouraged him to go see his physician.

"Those darn doctors charge too much," he said. "You're better off buying some snake oil from one of those travelin' salesmen."

The rancher strode out to his barn to feed his cattle. Like the aged man, the old corral had seen better days. Boards were missing, and the fence posts were leaning over. Instead of fixing the fence, the frugal rancher had set an electric wire around the inside to keep his cows in the pen. While he poured range cubes into troughs scattered around his corral, he accidentally tripped and touched the electric wire. A jolt of electricity pulsed through his body. The current threw him to the ground.

When he got up, he noticed something. Although sore, he felt a renewed sense of energy. Somehow, the electric shock had put a little spring in his step. The rancher brushed it off, finished his work and soon forgot about the whole ordeal.

Time passed. The stubborn old cowpuncher could barely make it to the corral each morning without gasping for air. Once again, he stumbled and touched the electric wire. After the current surged through his body, he felt better again. His shortness of breath improved. The rancher realized he was on to something. The shock gave him energy, helped him breathe better, and made him feel twenty years younger.

The resourceful senior ran the electric wire through the kitchen window to the dining room table. Every morning, he'd have his coffee, rub liniment on his joints, and grab the wire. After the shock wore off, he felt energized, ready to take on the day.

"It's my shock therapy," joked the unbending rancher.

This odd practice went on for months until the man was hospitalized for the first time in his life.

The cardiologist looked at his electrocardiogram with disbelief. "Have you been feeling tired or experiencing shortness of breath?"

The Texan confessed everything to the doctor: his self-prescribed shock therapies, the electric wire on the kitchen table, and his renewed sense of energy.

"You have atrial fibrillation. Your diseased heart is beating out of rhythm," said the cardiologist. "That's why you're feeling tired and short of breath. You need a cardioversion and a pacemaker."

The do-it-yourself rancher had been giving himself homemade cardioversions. By holding onto the hot electric wire, he shocked his heart back into rhythm. What the willful man didn't know could have hurt him. Pressing the reset button on the heart's electrical system can be dangerous: sometimes the shock makes the old ticker stop ticking—forever.

Define the Problem

Let me ask you, does your heart beat out of rhythm? Do you sense something wrong with your life? The first step to wholeness begins with recognizing we have a problem.

We must give the old cowpoke some credit. He recognized he had a problem, but he endangered his life with his homemade remedy.

If we're honest with ourselves, we are like the old rancher. We approach our lives with a *God, I've got this* mentality. We sense something is wrong, yet we can't pinpoint the problem. While we self-prescribe our own remedies, our diseased hearts beat out of rhythm. Let's not risk our future. Let's place our hearts in the competent hands of the One who can make us whole.

Put It in the Great Physician's Hands

The Great Physician knows our needs, has the answer and sees the best way to cure our maladies. Instead of trying a do-it-yourself remedy, experience His encouragement, His enlightenment, and His empowerment. The Great Physician waits, willing and able to heal.

We can come to Him, without even fully understanding our own problem. Grace is simple. God does for us what we cannot do for ourselves. We need to stop trying to fix it in our strength. We need to consult with the Great Physician.

"Come to Me, all who are weary and heavy-laden, and I will give you rest." [2]

*Good health and good sense
are two of life's greatest blessings.*
—Publilius Syrus

Chapter 3

THE MANDOLIN PLAYER

Courage to Do While You Can

W e should do what we can while we can do it, because a day will come when we can't.

The pallbearers laid their bouquets on the pine box, tears falling on the white rose petals. The ushers lowered the woman's casket into the ground while her husband squeezed the hands of their two children. They stood like statues as the sound of fresh dirt thudded on the box holding their loved one. After the service, the crowd dwindled and blended in among the gravestones. I watched the family linger at the grave, holding on to the moment. I wondered how someone could move forward after losing a spouse of twenty years.

He knew when they were dating this time would come, but his love outweighed the cruel reality. They married knowing her ailment would eventually cut her life short. Fortunately, Amanda lived longer than her doctors predicted. I didn't know her well, but I had to attend her funeral. I longed to hear her strum the mandolin once more.

She played the mandolin during our church services. Sometimes, her playing was off key and out of sync, but Amanda didn't seem to care.

In the past, I had nitpicked her performance. I also play the mandolin. From the stage, she would strum the strings, fake chords, and smile even when her disease made her cough.

The Dash in Between

Leaving her graveside, I stopped by some monuments and read their inscriptions. Out of the corner of my eye, I saw another freshly dug grave. I noticed there were two stones, but only one burial site. Filled with curiosity, I walked over to read the epitaph. One stone recorded a date of birth and a time of death, separated by a dash. The other marker was incomplete, having only the birthdate followed by the dash. The unfinished gravestone signified someone still on their life's journey.

I contemplated my own mortality, fixing my eyes on the little line. I thought of the significance of that little line. The dash represents the in-between. Memories. Failures. Successes. Relationships. Experiences. Joys. Pain.

I looked again at the first stone. I noticed something I had not recognized at first. The deceased person had died at the age of four. The epitaph read: *It's not the number, but the depth of years that makes life worth living.*

A thought crossed my mind. Why didn't I play the mandolin up on the stage? I could play circles around Amanda, yet she showed courage, while excuses filled my mind. I was shackled by my cell phone. Someone from the hospital calls every five minutes. I could never be on stage because of my ringing phone—or could I?

What to Do

I realized the difference between Amanda and me. She did not let excuses get in the way. She did what she could, while she could do it. And she did it to the best of her ability. She knew time was both precious and fleeting. She knew the day would soon come when she couldn't play her mandolin on stage. Time wouldn't allow her to polish her skills. *Now* was her opportunity. *Today* was her day to play. She didn't let her lack of musical skill and her health challenges inhibit her ability to sing, worship, and express thankfulness.

The One Certainty

Amanda had been given a unique gift. She knew her life would be short because of her chronic disease. She chose to live her life to the fullest and to pack as much as possible into every day.

Like Amanda, every person has an appointed time—a day coming when we will take our last breath. But what happens in the between—in the little dash chiseled into our gravestone—makes all the difference. If you're reading this, then your epitaph is incomplete. Inhale. You're still living in the dash.

Why Not Now

We know our time is fleeting but we procrastinate. We make excuses. We put off until tomorrow what should be done today. Then we spiritualize our indifference. We say things like, *I don't feel led to do that, such and such is not my spiritual gift* or *God hasn't called me.*

All the while, time passes. The urgent things of our day drown out the significant. Too often, we don't recognize how much time we have missed until the door of opportunity closes. Only then do we recognize our mistake. We pine with regret, calling to mind the things we could have done.

Take Advantage of Your Opportunities.

We should stop making excuses and do what we can do now, before it's too late. Most of us feel defeated by the things we can't do. Instead, we should focus on the activities we can do. There's still time. We can listen. We can learn. We can encourage. We can pray. We can worship. We can forgive. We can give. We can receive. We can love. We can rest. We can be like Amanda.

Play Your Mandolin

What is *your* mandolin? Think of the one thing you should be doing. Can you identify a God-given passion that stirs your soul?

We shouldn't wait for perfection, paralyzed by the fear of poor performance. We don't have to worry about what our critics may say. What really counts, more than what we do, is who we do it for. Amanda did not play her instrument to impress others. She did not perform for her own enjoyment. Amanda strummed her strings as an act of worship. She performed for one audience: the Throne of Heaven.

Whatever we do, we should do it while we can and do it for the right reasons. If God has planted the desire in our heart, if the goal will honor Him, and if we have the opportunity, we should do it. We must seize the moment before it's too late. Let's play our mandolin while we're still in the dash.

"Today, if you hear his voice, do not harden your hearts."[3]

Today's excuses are tomorrow's regrets dressed in disguise.

—Steven Furtick

Chapter 4
A LONG WAY FROM LILONGWE
Courage to See Others

I n 2004, I met a boy who challenged my views on suffering. We were on a mission trip, traveling into Mozambique.

Matt, our team leader, crammed us into the back of his Range Rover and drove hours down bumpy trails. Our destination was an isolated village somewhere in Mozambique. There, we planned to help a small, but growing church. After being jostled around for what seemed an eternity, we arrived at our destination

Matt opened the tailgate and let us out. "We can only get out here once a year. In the rainy season, it's impossible to drive down those trails."

I jumped out of the Range Rover, covered in sweat, feeling like a wet pair of shoes prematurely pulled out of a dryer. Refreshed by the wind, I took in the view of the mountains in the distance. In contrast, scores of mud houses covered with grass roofs scattered the landscape. There was no electricity. No running water. No signs of Western civilization. There were no roads, only small foot trails snaking off in all directions. We had arrived at the end of the earth.

Matt smiled. "It's a long way from Lilongwe. What do you guys think?"

I noticed two green flags flying over the largest house in the village. "Who lives there? The mayor?"

Matt, a seasoned missionary, shook his head. "No. That's the witch doctor's house. The green flags are his calling card."

I shivered, expecting a tribal warrior to jump out at us, mask and spear in hand. Matt reassured us. "Never mind the witch doctor. You'll never see him."

We exhaled in relief. Matt gave a mischievous smile and pointed at a grove of trees. "Keep your eyes peeled for the *Gulewamkulu*. They come from the graveyard. They're natives who dress up to scare people. They call themselves the *Gulewam*. The big dance."

We watched a crowd gather around us, women and barefoot children wearing tattered clothes. Matt pointed to some other children, not more than seven years of age, carrying babies in little papooses on their backs. "They're raising their younger siblings. Their parents have died of HIV."

Two African toddlers screamed and pulled away from their mothers, shouting, "Mzungu. Mzungu." One mother pulled her little one closer, reassuring him we meant no harm.

I gave Matt a puzzled look. "What's going on?"

Matt laughed. "Some of these kids have never seen a white person. Mzungu means *white man*. They're scared because people say white people will take them away and eat them."

Within minutes, a large group of villagers assembled. Matt started the church service under a tree. We sang, danced, and gave a basic presentation of the Good News.

Forty people responded to a simple message of salvation. No hype. No gimmicks. No hoopla. Filled with joy, everyone sang and danced some more. I stepped back for a moment, taking it all in. These poor, isolated Africans experienced something that most of Western Christianity, with all its money, programs, and resources, couldn't. Happiness. Abundance. Togetherness. Fellowship. Joy. Courage.

I noticed a group of kids circling around a boy about eight years of age. At first, I thought they were playing a game, but the boy in the middle tried to run away. The others chased after him, laughing, and pointing. A large scarf covered the young boy's head.

Curious, I walked toward them, approached the child and removed the scarf covering his head. When I peered behind the veil, I withdrew in horror. I realized why the other children were picking on the boy.

A football-sized mass protruded from his neck, pushing his head sideways, eroding through the skin. Flies swarmed over the weeping, proud flesh. Fortunately, the drainage and dirt formed a cake-like dressing that covered the raw open wound. The boy, too frightened to speak and too scared to run, bowed his head in humiliation. He looked at me, his deep brown eyes whispering a cry of desperation.

I had been so focused on the little boy I didn't realize a crowd had gathered around us. The boy's mother, thinking her son was in danger, quickly came to his rescue. I looked into the mother's face. She wore the same hopeless expression as her son. "What is his name?"

Fortunately, Matt arrived at the scene and translated her response. "Kalikoka."

I laughed. "Sounds like Coca Cola to me. Did they name him after a soft drink?"

Matt wasn't laughing. "In Chichewa, Kalikoka means *alone.*"

The mother told us how the university hospital in Lilongwe had given them no hope. The boy had a Burkitt's lymphoma—a tumor that could have melted away with several rounds of chemotherapy.

Unfortunately, Kalikoka lived on the wrong continent. In southern Africa, most families live on less than two dollars a month. Even if they could afford Western therapies, the drugs to cure his disease weren't available. They had no access to clean water, let alone advanced medical therapies.

The mother pointed to the green flags. Matt looked bewildered and stood silent, trying to absorb everything she was saying. In a broken voice, he translated, "She took him to the witch doctor."

They had heard in their village that this witch doctor had a cure for what ailed the boy. So, they walked forty miles to the green flagged hut. When I heard the mother's story, I didn't know whom I was sadder for—the mother or the boy. I tried to imagine the helpless mother, doing what she could for her dying son. Her love was so great; she would've swallowed fire if the witch doctor had told her to.

Whether in Africa or Alabama, a mother's love compels her to do everything possible for her child. A mother never gives up. She will leave no stone unturned. Tired of covering her child's distorted body and hiding the humiliation, Kalikoka's mother decided to do something—even if her efforts were a long shot.

We said our goodbyes to the village and offered the two a ride home. On the long trip back to Lilongwe, we explained to them how to receive God's gift of eternal life. And with great joy, they did. We dropped them off in their village, wondering what would happen to the young boy.

Several weeks later, Kalikoka died. Matt and his wife attended his funeral. The boy's relatives, who also happened to be the tribe's chiefs, were moved by the compassion of the missionaries. They received the gospel and built a church that bears the boy's name. They call it the Coca-Cola Church.

Today, over a decade later, there are several churches, born out of a dying boy's unexplainable tragedy. God used Kalikoka's suffering for a greater purpose.

Seeing Versus Perceiving

We live in a world of distractions that keep us from truly seeing the needs of others. We see with our eyes, but we don't see with our hearts. Jesus modeled an awareness, a focus, and a passion to see people as *people*. What about us? What distracts us from seeing as Jesus did? Perhaps we're preoccupied by our computers or phones. We may have no margin in our schedules. We're busy but barren. Sometimes, we suffer with our own afflictions. How can we help someone else when we have so many issues of our own to work through?

If we have the Spirit of God living within us, then we have the capacity to see others. We find what we look for. Every day, God gives us opportunities to see, perceive, and engage. We must stop, open the eyes of our hearts, and listen to the quiet whisper of the Spirit. Our destiny and that of others hang in the balance. Could it be that our awareness could change the outcome of a situation?

Our Mutual Benefit

Seeing and engaging others may be more about us than the one needing to be touched. In our distraction, we fail to recognize that the exact thing we need flows from helping others. When we give, we live. If we're experiencing loneliness, we should befriend someone. If we're afflicted with a health issue, we can reach out to someone with physical need. We can change our focus. What would I have missed out on if I hadn't noticed the boy being bullied? If I hadn't followed my curiosity, I would've missed out on one of my biggest blessings. Could our distraction rob us of joy, peace, and the fulfillment for which we were created?

But God often places the solutions to our issues right in front of us, in the form of distractions. When we become aware of the needs of others, when we see, perceive, and act, our hope flourishes. A miracle occurs for both the giver and receiver. Our troubles lighten. Our perspective changes. We ourselves experience the emotional, spiritual, and physical healing we need.

His Ways Versus Our Ways

If I had been given the opportunity, I would've written a different ending to Kalikoka's story. My tale would've included a dramatic healing, a long life, and a bucket full of blessings for this African boy.

However, God's ways are different than our ways. God chose a different resolution for Kalikoka on this side of eternity. We must not forget the story is God's story, not ours. God invites us to participate in a drama crafted to display His goodness, adequacy, and power in indescribable ways.

On this occasion, God brought a helpless doctor, a dying child and some dedicated missionaries together on the backside of Mozambique to remind us of something. No matter where we are or who we are, He sees, He knows, He cares, and He provides. We are not alone. God can take our afflictions, no matter how difficult or challenging, and weave them into His greater story. Do you believe in His sovereign goodness?

> *"'For my thoughts are not your thoughts, neither are your ways my ways,' declares the Lord. 'As the heavens are higher than the earth, so are my ways higher than your ways and my thoughts than your thoughts.'"* [4]

God moves in mysterious ways,
His wonders to perform.
He plants His footsteps in the sea
and rides upon the storm.

—William Cowper

Chapter 5

SELF-DESTRUCTIVE BEHAVIOR
Courage to Want to Get Well

B illy walked into the exam room, took off his denim jacket, and loosed the pearl snap buttons on his western shirt. "I used to rodeo. Then, ten years ago, a bull gored me in the stomach." He stretched out on the examination table. "The leakage goes everywhere. Stool oozes around the colostomy bag and burns my belly."

I removed the bag and saw his intestines discharge green fluid through a healed surgical scar. A fistula: a surgeon's worst nightmare.

In desperation he asked, "Can you help me? Everyone else says it can't be fixed. But, I'm losing weight and I can't work."

His scar-covered abdomen had lost its soft texture. Now his belly felt harder than concrete. "Billy, I bet your intestines are a matted mess of scar tissue. Sometimes, we get in there and can't distinguish one piece of bowel from the other."

He nodded his head. "I know. I've already had twelve surgeries, with six fistulas and six bowel obstructions. The last doctor told me I'm a walking time bomb."

"Why did you quit your last doctor?" I asked.

"I didn't. He wouldn't see me anymore. He said I was an impossible case."

With a discouraged and forlorn look in his eyes, he continued, "I have to keep going. I hope to work again one day and carry on a normal life."

I looked again at his stomach, the bag, and the scarred abdomen, imagining the intestines glued together in a matted mess. I reminded the cowboy that this was not my first rodeo either. "What makes you think another operation will work? You've already had twelve failures. What makes you think number thirteen will be any different than the others?"

Billy sighed. "Doctor, don't give up on me like everybody else. You're my only hope."

In the following days, I did my due diligence, obtaining old operative reports, ordering new tests, and visiting with Billy in the clinic for several weeks. I found the problem: a blocked intestine downstream that obstructed the flow of intestinal contents. I prepared Billy for a long, complicated surgery. With each visit, Billy displayed proper motivation and a desire to get better. After weeks of discussion, testing, and planning, we reached the day of Billy's surgery.

Billy's operation lasted six hours. I chipped through the concrete-like scar tissue in his abdomen, meticulously separating his intestines. We removed the part of the intestine that leaked to the outside without problems and fixed the blockage. Success. After finishing Billy's case, I gave myself a pat on the back. No complications. Finally, after decades, I sensed the feeling of accomplishment. I had arrived as a surgeon.

Over the next several days, we had trouble controlling Billy's pain. The nurses became worried about the dosage of narcotics we were giving him. With his long history of surgeries, I reminded them that Billy would have a high degree of tolerance to pain medications. Now, with his problem fixed, we could eventually wean him off his pain medicines as his body healed. I reassured myself that the cowboy's pain problems were temporary.

For the first few days, Billy progressed without any issues. Then late one evening, about 2 a.m., I received a frantic call from the nurse. "Doctor, bowel contents are seeping out of his incision. You need to come to the bedside."

I drove to the hospital, recalling every detail of Billy's procedure. I had performed a perfect operation. Yet for some unexplainable reason, guilt and regret filled my mind. I should've known better than to think I was better than his twelve previous surgeons. They also had problems with Billy.

I walked down the hallway to Billy's room questioning my judgement. *Perhaps I was too prideful, too confident of my abilities.* I thought of all the work, risk, and time I had expended. Billy was no better—maybe even worse—than before.

At three in the morning, the hallway was empty, quiet, and lonely. Like the vacant corridor, I felt hollow on the inside. The feeling intensified with each step closer to his room. Billy's door was partially open. I tiptoed in, trying not to make a disturbance. I thought Billy might be sleeping.

I couldn't believe what I saw next.

Billy had a sinister look on his face. He held a pocketknife. With it, he sawed on his incision. He cut away another stitch holding the muscle together. I heard a popping sound followed by the gushing of green fluid from his belly.

My frustration turned into anger. I watched him put down his knife and call for the nurse. "I need more pain medications. I can't stand it anymore."

Afraid I'd explode if I entered his room, I turned away before he saw me and walked back down the quiet hallway. I'd been tricked. Duped. Deceived. Like a violin virtuoso, Billy had played me like a worn-out fiddle. Sickness was just a game for Billy, a way to get high on pain meds, a means to fulfill his narcotic addiction. He never wanted to get well at all.

Medicine gives behavior like Billy's a name: *malingering*. Malingerers either pretend or make themselves sick for some type of secondary gain. Some enjoy the attention they get. Others want to dull the pain in their lives with medications. Sickness exists merely as a means to an end.

Who's the Fool?

You can double-cross your doctor. You can fool your friends, family, and even your pastor. But you can't fool God. Jesus sees what no one else can see. He perceives our motives, our will, and our selfish desires.

At the pool of Bethesda, Jesus asked an invalid a good question: *"Do you want to get well?"*[5] The beggar had been paralyzed for thirty-eight years. He sat, waiting for the waters to stir. He wanted to be the first to jump in the pool and be healed, but his paralysis held him back.

Living hand-to-mouth was the only life he knew. It's possible he had grown accustomed to his conditions. At least the beggar had some certainty in his uncertain existence. If he were healed, his whole way of life would change. He'd no longer live on the attention, sympathy, and generosity of others. He could no longer take from the givers. A pair of new legs would bring new challenges, new uncertainties, and new responsibilities.

Jesus probed the paralytic with a question. "Do you want to get well?" He wanted the disabled man to think about how his life would change if he received healing. Perhaps, like Billy, the disabled man did not desire to get better.

Self-Inflicted Wounds

Although unrecognized, most people possess some of Billy's self-destructive behavior. We are spiritual malingerers. We get comfortable living in our brokenness. We like the attention we receive when we're sick. We enjoy having our name on the prayer list. Rather than picking up our mat, trusting God's promises, walking in freedom and living in wholeness, we choose to remain broken. We malinger. The fringe benefits of being sick outweigh the risk of the unknown. Like Billy, we repeat the same cycle—over and over. We take the knife, stab ourselves and fail to become whole.

On the Mat

What paralyzes you? What disabling attitude keeps you on your mat? A laundry list of excuses hinders our progress: a history of abuse, a past relational wound, fear of failure, emotional neglect from a parent, sexual exploitation, a past regret, a guilty conscience. To break the cycle, you must do the very thing you fear. You must trust God, obey his commands and take a risk.

The road to healing is never easy. Ask the beggar at Bethesda. But God's power can be released when we obey. Impossible things can become possible.

Begin with Introspection

Let's consider the new challenges we'll have when our breakthrough comes. Are we ready to take on the risk, uncertainty, and change that comes with healing? If we take Jesus up on His offer, our lives will be transformed, but are we ready?

We should think about Jesus's compelling question. Do we really want to be healed? Wholeness requires adjustments on multiple levels, not just on the physical. Sometimes we need to change on the inside before we experience a physical breakthrough.

Claim His Promises

Once we've counted the cost and considered the new challenges ahead, what next? We believe His promise, and like the paralytic, we take Him up on his offer. We pick up our mats and walk. We start experiencing restoration from the inside out. Wholeness begins within and flows into every hidden crevice of our lives—body, soul, and spirit.

Let's not malinger. We don't have to wait around some pool for a mysterious stirring of magic water. Look up. Jesus offers the answer. He promises to make us whole.

"Then Jesus said to him, 'Get up! Pick up your mat and walk.'"[6]

"The greatest day in your life and mine is when we take total responsibility for our attitudes. That's the day we truly grow up."

—John C. Maxwell

Chapter 6

THINGS ARE NEVER
AS BAD AS THEY SEEM
Courage to Choose Peace

T he gynecologist called me to see an old patient with a new problem: a pelvic tumor.

I knew Maria well. Seven years before, I removed her colon cancer. When I walked into her room, her husband Rick met me at the door. He gave a sarcastic smile and laughed. "We haven't seen you in a while, Doctor."

We exchanged jokes while Maria lay on her hospital bed. She nervously punched buttons on the TV control. "The gynecologist says I have an ovarian mass. They think it's cancer. It started five days ago." Her husband's cell phone rang, interrupting Maria. She placed her hand on her stomach, winced in pain and snatched the phone from his hand. "Give me that."

The words *stressed out* could have been stamped on her forehead. Anyone could see she wasn't taking the news well.

Maria spoke into the phone. "I have cancer." Her lip quivered. Her voice cracked. "They're doing exploratory surgery in the morning."

Her phone interruption gave Rick a chance to talk. "Sorry, Doctor. My wife's normally sweeter than peach tea. She's got a lot on her mind."

Maria finished her call and gave the cell phone back to her husband. "Rick, your sister has the kids."

Puzzled, I asked them, "Whose kids?"

Maria sighed. "We're raising our grandkids till our daughter is released from prison. This is the worst time to get sick. They have basketball and soccer after school." A tear trickled down her cheek. "I never thought I'd be raising kids again."

I struggled to steer Maria into discussing her medical history. She talked about everything but her physical ailments—family problems, financial burdens.

Finally, after getting the information I needed, I sat at the foot of the bed. "Maria, most of the things we worry about never happen. And if they do, they're never as bad as we imagine. Don't you remember what happened seven years ago?"

Maria nodded her head. "Of course, I do. You removed my colon cancer. The chemo was the hardest part. I lost my hair."

I nodded. "You lost your hair—for a little while, but you didn't lose your life. You suffered only for a season." I looked at Maria and realized my pep talk was working. "Did things turn out as badly as you thought?"

Maria exhaled. "You're right. I was a basket case when you told me I had colon cancer. But God saw me through. And you are right: things don't turn out like I imagine. I beat cancer the first time, and I can beat it again."

Rick chimed in, "Maria, don't worry about the grandkids. If you get sick, God will provide someone to take care of them. God always, *somehow*, works everything out for us." I sat and listened to them recall all the good things they had experienced. While they counted their blessings, Maria's countenance changed. Her attitude made an about-face with one little comment: *"Most of the things we really worry about never happen. And if they do, they're never as bad as we imagine."*

I walked out of their hospital room, marveling at their change in focus, and I thought to myself. *I'll have to use that line more often.* Maria's irritability, pain, and discouragement had been replaced with peace, joy, and thankfulness. I introduced a better way of thinking. They did the rest. One little statement initiated a whole cascade of good thoughts. One comment changed Maria's outlook.

Don't Let Skin Get in the Way of a Diagnosis

The next morning, we took Maria to the operating room. We hoped for the best but prepared for the worst. Would we encounter a "peek and shriek" situation? A belly laden with metastatic ovarian cancer? A large malignant mass? Or would we find something else? We were surprised to find a large ovary, filled with blood, twisted on itself. An ovarian torsion. No malignancy. She received a quick, straightforward surgery. Upon closing her abdomen, we laughed and reminded ourselves, "Boring is good, and boring and fast is even better."

You Must Draw It Out

Typically, we think peace occurs in the absence of adversity. Peace equals no problems plus no pain. Conversely, the peace Jesus gives transcends our situations. God's tranquility isn't grounded in conditions or based on comfort.

"Peace I leave with you; my peace I give you. I do not give to you as the world gives. Do not let your hearts be troubled and do not be afraid." [7]

Have we considered how our problems can fuel our experience of the peace Jesus promised?

Don't Pray for Peace

We don't need to pray for peace. We already have it. If we have received Christ and the Holy Spirit abides within, then we possess an ocean of calmness. Instead of asking for peace, we should draw upon what we have already received. A better response comes by praying, "God, help me to use the peace you have promised."

Our Difficulties Are Never as Bad as We Think

When going through trouble, our mind multiplies our troubles and erases our blessings. We create problems and situations that may never happen. We imagine the worst possible scenario. We *let* our hearts trouble us with doubt, fear, and discouragement. We allow worry to creep in and steal the peace Jesus has deposited.

When worry invades our thinking, we must remind ourselves: *things are never as bad as they appear. God is in control. He has a plan.* God will either deliver us from our circumstance or give us the courage to endure whatever comes our way. Either way, God has our back. He guarantees it. So, why worry?

We can withdraw on the peace we've received and be thankful. We can remember all the ways God has come through in the past. Let's encourage ourselves with the promises given in scripture. Let's focus on helping someone worse off than us. Nothing changes our attitude more than taking our eyes off our situation and focusing on God's promises.

Don't Borrow Trouble

No thief is greater than the one called borrowed trouble. He fills our mind with things which *may* happen. Borrowed trouble tricks us into pondering the imponderable. He prods us to meditate on our problems. All the while, he steals our joy. Once we're distracted, He robs our tranquility, replacing it with worry, dread, and fear. He swindles the Christian out of their greatest assets: the ability to hear God's voice and the blessing of abiding in His presence. He knows that taking those abilities today hinders our ability to prepare for tomorrow. Once we've lost our bearings, defeat is possible.

We mustn't befriend borrowed trouble or allow him to enter our mind. Jesus reminded us that today has enough trouble to focus on. He promises us tomorrow will take care of itself. Instead of stressing about what may happen in the future, let's concentrate on what we need to do today. Why worry about tomorrow if we can do something about it today?

Meditation Drives Worry Away

Our thoughts are like a container stuffed with all kinds of notions. If we fill our mind with truth, there will be no space for worry, fear and other defeating emotions. Meditation places God's promises in our thoughts and consciousness.

When worry fills our minds, we can meditate on what is noble, right, good, pure, lovely, and excellent. We can choose to fill our mind with God's blessings. We can be thankful in our circumstances. When we do, those thoughts of worry flee from our mind. When we have replaced our fear with peace, there is no room for worry.

Take a scripture and write it down where you'll see it often: on a computer screen, in a cell-phone, on a 3 x 5 card. Memorize the verse, read it aloud, and stress the different words in the promise.

This process of bathing the mind with scripture keeps your focus on God and His promises. The result is the peace of God that transcends understanding.

Spiritual Amnesia

If we are not careful, we can focus on the wrong things. We forget God's promises and remember our problems. Reverse your thinking. When pushing through challenging circumstances, we can consider God's faithfulness—the ways He showed up in the past. The fractured relationships He has restored, the answered prayers, the unexpected blessings that appeared out of nowhere. How about the people who were there to encourage us in past trials?

When we reflect on God's character, faithfulness, and intervention in our past, our problems are soon forgotten. When worry knocks on our door to threaten our peace, let's just close the door. We don't have to let it into our minds. Let's not surrender the blessing of calm contentment we've received. Instead, let's meditate on God's unchanging promises. No one can take away our peace, but we can give it away. Let's be thankful, and most of all, choose peace.

"You will keep in perfect peace those whose minds are steadfast, because they trust in you." [8]

We are not called to be burden-bearers,
but cross-bearers and light-bearers. We
must cast our burdens on the Lord.

—Corrie ten Boom

Chapter 7

ANGEL KISSES

Courage to Love Unconditionally

S haron walked into the exam room with her grandchild in tow. The toddler began the conversation. A red stain circled her mouth, making her look like a clown. She removed her lollipop and held up three fingers. "My name is Claire, and I'm this many."

Sharon sat, picked up Claire, and produced a smile only found in grandmothers. Then, matter-of-factly, she said, "I have Von Recklinghausen's disease."

I nodded. She resembled an alien from a far-away planet. Grotesque squid-like tentacles protruded from her skin.

"I can see that. Your picture should be in a medical textbook. What can I do for you?"

"My bumps are bothering me. Can you take them off?"

Puzzled, I looked at the hundreds of fleshy projections. "That's impossible. I can't perform a skin transplant."

Sharon shook her head. "No. That's not what I'm asking for. I don't want *all* of them removed. I like my warts." She rubbed the fleshy bumps growing from her skin. "Just remove these three on my back. They bleed every time I put my pants on."

I sighed in relief. "Oh, I see."

"Doctor, I have had this disease all my life. God gave it to me. I wouldn't want you to remove my bumps, even if you could." Sharon bounced Claire on her knee. "All my life, people have been afraid to touch me. They thought I had some contagious disease." She paused and kissed her granddaughter on the cheek. "When I was a child, parents would grab their children and walk the other way. I heard them whisper to their kids, 'Stay away from that girl. Don't touch her. If you do, your skin will be covered in warts.'"

Sharon told how people treated her like an outcast, judging her for a condition she could not change. She was a modern-day leper. Someone untouchable. I wondered what emotional and psychological scars were buried deep inside, below her skin bumps and protrusions.

My thoughts stirred my emotions, the first being anger. Society failed to accept her because she was different. Sorrow quickly followed. Sharon lived sixty-four years with a condition she had no power to change. I wanted to ask Sharon how living with such a visible syndrome affected her sense of self-worth. But I didn't have to.

I looked at Claire, bouncing on Sharon's knee. She rubbed her sticky hand over the fleshy tentacles on Sharon's face. "Grandma's bumps are angel kisses."

I saw Sharon smile, her face now checkered with red lollipop stains. My feelings were replaced with a deep sense of joy. Sharon received something from her granddaughter that many never experience:

unconditional love. Little Claire accepted Grandma—as is—without reservation.

Angel Kisses

If only we had the courage to see like Sharon's granddaughter—below the skin. Sometimes, it takes child-like vision to see beneath the surface to glimpse into the heart—to see people as God sees them. After preaching the Sermon on the Mount, Jesus walked down the mountain and encountered a leper.

> *A man with leprosy came and knelt before him and said, "Lord, if you are willing you can make me clean." Jesus reached out his hand and touched the man, "I am willing," he said. "Be clean!"* [9]

People Long to Be Touched

How many people cross our path every day who have never been touched? Some people's needs are easy to spot, like the bumps covering Sharon's skin. They wear their afflictions on the surface where everyone can see them. Loneliness. Fear. Anger. They clothe themselves with the *don't touch me, I'm hurting* attitude. Others hide their issues below the surface. On the outside, everything looks great. They dress themselves up in success, the material, and busyness. They wear the *got it all-together* garb. However, deep inside, below the layers of self-preservation, their hidden pain festers.

If we're honest, each of us longs for a touch from heaven. We long for someone to call our blemishes *angel kisses*. We need God's hand to reach out in our need and proclaim, "I am willing. Be clean." We need to be touched and we need to touch others with acceptance, forgiveness, and love.

See as Jesus Saw

The crowds following Jesus down the mountain didn't distract Him from His mission to touch others. The Master had no concern about what others would think. When Jesus saw the leper, He didn't see him as a risk or an interruption. He was not concerned about exposure to a contagious disease or becoming ceremonially unclean. Jesus didn't ask, *"If I get involved, what could I lose?"* Jesus didn't look at the leper and blame him personally for his malady. Jesus didn't look at the sores on his body and say, *"He deserves to have leprosy. He's paying for his sins."*

The Lord had a different view of the situation. Jesus saw a person, someone who desperately needed to be touched. Like Sharon's grandchild, Jesus saw beneath the surface. He saw the heart.

When we see others, do we have a skin-deep attitude, or do we look deeper? Can we see those *angel kisses* in people? We find what we are looking for. The sufferings of others are part of God's purpose—not only for the afflicted but also for us. Our response to other's circumstances often tells more about our attitudes than those who are suffering. Could those who are different be part of a heavenly test? An opportunity to respond like Jesus?

Do as Jesus Did

Jesus saw below the surface, but He didn't stop there. Filled with compassion and courage, Jesus acted upon what he saw. He touched the leper without fear or hesitation. Unaware of the power channeled through her touch, Claire accepted and loved her grandmother. When others saw Sharon's grotesque deformities, Claire saw *angel kisses.* Claire's hands, covered with lollipop juice, touched a deep need in her grandmother—the desire to be accepted and loved, just like the rest of us, warts and all.

But How?

If the Spirit of Christ lives in us, then we can see and do as Jesus did. The same power that recognized the need, reached out with compassion, and risked touching the untouchable, lives within us. Are we drawing on our source of power? We must abide in the presence of the living God who lives with us—the Spirit received when we accepted Christ. We draw upon the power that does immeasurably more than we can ask or think. We can depend upon the presence of the one who works in and through our lives. God intends for us to be channels for His transforming touch. Are you ready and willing to touch others?

> *A man with leprosy came and knelt before him and said, "Lord, if you are willing, you can make me clean." Jesus reached out his hand and touched the man. "I am willing," he said. "Be clean!"* [10]

Faith
makes all things possible.
Love
makes all things easy.
—Dwight L. Moody

Chapter 8
A TOUGH PILL TO SWALLOW
Courage to Die

H enry walked into the exam room, leaned forward, and put his hand on his chest. "It hurts when I swallow."
I listened while the thought crossed my mind, "*Problems swallowing in a ninety-year-old. Not a good sign.*"

His endoscopy confirmed my suspicion. A large tumor closed off his esophagus.

I gave Henry his options. "Considering your age, medical problems, and advanced disease, you're not a candidate for surgery. You should consider chemotherapy, radiation, a feeding tube, and a stent to open up your swallowing tube."

Henry sat quietly, taking everything in, weighing his options. I waited, watching his expressions change. He smiled and then told his story.

"I've survived two heart attacks, a minor stroke, colon cancer, and the passing of my wife. I'm ready."

"Ready for radiation?" I asked.

"No doctor, I'm ready to see my loved ones in heaven."

"But what about treatment?"

"Sir, I have pastored a small congregation for four decades. Our church has dwindled to only a handful of people. Most of my friends and family have already passed on. My time has come. I have finished my race."

I gave Henry the details of what to expect with his disease, making sure he understood the consequences of his decision.

"Cancer of the esophagus leads to a gruesome death. Your body will waste away from progressive malnutrition. When the esophagus closes off completely, you will not be able to swallow your spit. You will drown in your saliva."

"I understand," he said. "God will give me the grace to endure it. I believe that to be absent from this body is to be present with the Lord."

Henry stayed true to his faith.

I walked with Henry throughout his journey, seeing him often on return visits to the office. I watched his body wither away over several months, but I never heard him complain.

On his last visit, he sat in a chair and spit saliva into a cup. At this point, nothing could pass down into his stomach. "Thanks Doc, for not making me go through all that chemo and X-ray treatment."

Every step of the way, he found God's generous supply of grace helping him in his time of need. He never complained, because everything he needed had been provided for him. He continued to pastor his congregation until the day he passed away. However, Henry didn't die the way I expected, suffocating from his own saliva, shriveling from esophageal cancer. He died from another heart attack while sleeping.

At his funeral, I realized the simplicity of Henry's faith. He consumed grace in small doses. Henry drew on God's provision each day. Every new challenge with his sickness brought a fresh supply of mercy.

Don't Let Worry Rob You of Peace and Joy

Everybody wants to experience heaven, but no one enjoys the process of getting there. Dying involves pain. Dwelling on future suffering borrows problems from tomorrow, robbing us of peace and joy in the present. Imponderable questions race through our minds, stealing our tranquility and happiness. How will we endure the pain? Will we have the courage to die with dignity? The *what ifs* begin to fill our thoughts, hindering our ability to enjoy the present.

We must remember how God supplies the riches of His grace. He deposits it for our use in our time of need.

God Provides Grace as We Need It

God doesn't allow us to store His provision for a rainy day. Grace cannot be hoarded. We cannot draw out of the bank account of God's riches before we need it. Like the manna in the wilderness, we can only receive God's unmerited favor one day, one moment, one step at a time. Sufficient for each day are the blessings to meet our present needs. God provides grace for every need—past, present, and future—at exactly the moment we need it.

Learn to Draw on God's Grace, Moment by Moment

God provided manna for His people after they crossed the Red Sea. The provision supplied enough for each day—no more, no less. New mercies every morning. The provision had no benefit until someone gathered and consumed it. The manna from heaven needed to be appropriated. Every day, every moment, we must draw upon what God has already given us. We shouldn't get ahead of God's provision. We can't pay for tomorrow's troubles with the grace received today. When we need more grace, God's generosity will supply it. We should focus on consuming our blessings in the present moment.

Endurance, faith, wisdom, courage, peace, love, and patience—everything has already been deposited into our spiritual bank. We can use it when the need arises.

God completed His work on the cross. Everything needed for our journey has been given. Like Henry, lean upon the vast supply of grace. It's always enough, always on time, and always available. Miraculously, God's sufficient provision will be there in our time of need.

"Therefore let us approach the throne of grace with boldness, so that we may receive mercy and find grace to help us at the proper time." [11]

*God never made a promise
that was too good to be true.*

—Dwight L. Moody

Chapter 9

LESSONS LEARNED

Courage to Look at Ourselves Objectively

T he nurses wheeled a dirty cowboy into the trauma room. They strapped Rowdy down to keep him from moving.

He was naked, save for one feature of clothing: a pair of dirty leather boots stuck out from under the sheets.

"Don't touch my boots," he screamed. "Those cost me three hundred dollars."

I watched outside the trauma room, giving the nurses time to do their assessment, looking at his vital signs.

I walked in. The head nurse looked at me and smirked. "They picked him up at the rodeo. He was impaled in the leg by a bull's horn."

He smiled at me and crossed his boots.

"Hey Doc," he said. "I'm all right. This ain't the first time I've danced with a bull."

I examined the cowboy from head to toe. Scars covered his body.

"How old are you?" I asked.

"Thirty-nine going on twenty."

A scar ran from his left chin to his scalp.

"How'd you get that scar on your face?"

"That bull's name was 'Looking for Trouble.'" The cowboy laughed.

"Same with the left shoulder?" I said, noticing a scar that shot from his shoulder to the elbow.

"Nope, got thrown from a bronco down in Tucson. He stepped on me."

"And what was the bronco's name?"

"Don't remember," he said. "But they screwed some metal in my arm."

I palpated his abdomen, covered by a large midline scar. Before I could ask, he interrupted.

"Spent a month in the ICU with that one. Got attacked by another bull. He trampled all over me. Those clowns saved my life. The docs took out my spleen, patched up my liver and did some fancy operation on my pancreas." He grinned. "But I hung on for eight seconds. Came in third. All the dang prize money went to doctor bills."

I looked down at his leg. A large gash exposed his knee joint. The tendons and muscles were severed. I could see the blood vessels exposed in the depths of the wound. Just another millimeter deeper and the bull could have claimed the victory.

I made a sarcastic remark, trying to get his attention. "Good thing you were wearing those boots."

"Yep," said Rowdy. "They're my luckiest pair. I never get on a bull without 'em."

I did a double take. "Have you noticed a pattern here?"

After an uncomfortable pause, he smiled back at me. "Doc, I need to learn to ride a little better."

Possibilities Not Problems

Every circumstance—good or bad—presents us with new possibilities. Our trials are occasions to learn, grow, and to show God's adequacy. Even temptations can be wonderful opportunities to do good.

Like Rowdy, we often lack insight into the real source of our problems. We live in denial. We repeat the same blunders over and over, expecting a different outcome. We fail to learn from our mistakes. If only we could see our circumstances in an objective manner.

Another Set of Eyes

We need to allow others to examine our lives. Sometimes, they can see what we cannot. They have insight into how we can get out of our unhealthy cycles that hinder growth, healing and maturity. A trusted friend often looks at our problems through objective lenses. In love, they can show us some ways we can progress, break our negative patterns and heal painful habits. If you repeat the same life choices, don't expect something different to happen. Find a friend who will tell you the truth in love. Listen and learn.

Passing the Test, Learning the Lesson

Are we teachable? If we don't learn from our experiences, we're bound to repeat them. God's children don't fail tests. Instead, God makes them repeat the test over and over and over, until finally, they pass.

> *"Search me, O God, and know my heart; test me and know my anxious thoughts. See if there is any offensive way in me and lead me in the way everlasting."*[12]

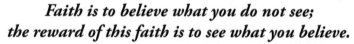

Faith is to believe what you do not see;
the reward of this faith is to see what you believe.

—Saint Augustine

Chapter 10

SHE'S PERFECT

Courage to See the Unseen

A gloom fell over the emergency room. Personnel adjusted the ventilator, shot x-rays, and clicked away on their computers. A teenage girl lay on the trauma room gurney, her naked body caked in blood, dirt, and glass. She tried to outrun a train. The train won.

I pinched her elbow with my fingernails, leaving a deep depression in her skin. She did not draw away from the pain, a sign of brain death. Her right femur, broken on impact, pierced through the skin of her thigh. Small pieces of broken glass were embedded in her face and neck.

I looked at the squiggly tracing lines on the monitor. Normal vital signs. Her pulse, blood pressure, and oxygen levels were perfect. I examined her eyes, shining a bright light in her pupils.

"The pupils are fixed and dilated," I said in a loud voice.

"Any signs of brain activity?" asked one of the nurses clicking boxes on the computer screen. Distracted by the noise, commotion, and the computer, she didn't understand my comment.

In a louder voice, I repeated myself. "The pupils are fixed and dilated."

The neurosurgeon entered the room, looked at her CAT scan, and confirmed what everyone suspected.

"There's nothing I can do. She's brain dead. Her brain is swollen, but there's nothing to operate on. I've got another subdural to drain at the other hospital. Can you talk with the family about organ donation?" he asked.

One by one, personnel left the room and moved on to the next trauma patient. Another dose of adrenaline awaited them next door. I remained, finishing up some details. The bustling noises were soon replaced by the rhythmical sound of the breathing machine.

I gathered my thoughts, preparing for the family waiting outside. *How can I tell them their child is brain dead and will never live a normal life?*

Before I could answer my own question, the chaplain brought the family into the room. Overwhelmed, they said little at first.

Then the girl's father asked, "Can we touch her?"

I nodded my head.

Her mother grabbed the girl's limp hand and whispered in her ear. "Sweetheart, everything is gonna be okay. Everyone's here. We love you."

I stumbled through introductions and did my best to explain the girl's prognosis. My words were ineffective. They didn't seem to hear what I was saying. Instead, they moved toward their daughter's bedside and watched her life slip away. Seeing is believing, they say.

"Her name is Kendall," said the mother. "She's been accepted to medical school."

I listened while the family told me all about her accomplishments.

The more I listened, the more they talked. I realized I had answered my own question. People don't care how much you know until they know how much you care. The best approach involved listening to the family's stories, helping them move towards closure. Before they finished, Kendall's vital signs deteriorated. The brain swelling slowed the pace of her heart. Her organ systems were shutting down. Soon, Kendall would cross over into eternity.

I finished my paperwork and watched the family circle the bedside. They held hands and prayed. I listened to them while working on the computer. Some expressed their disappointment and sorrow. Others thanked God. Still others, shocked from the whole incident, were speechless. During their prayer, the monitors sounded an alarm. I walked over, silenced the distracting clamor and headed back to my computer screen.

A hand touched me on the shoulder.

"Doctor, would you pray with us?" asked Kendall's grandmother. For a moment, I hesitated. Reluctantly, I joined hands with the circle while Grandma prayed. "Thank you, Father; now, she's perfect."

Stunned by her prayer, I opened my eyes and peeked at Kendall, expecting to see something different. During the prayer, the zigzag lines representing her heart rhythm turned into flat ones on the monitor. Kendall had crossed over. I tried to let go of the hands holding mine, but they seemed to be glued together. I couldn't let go, yet I had to pronounce the patient.

While everyone's eyes were closed, I reexamined her body, while still holding hands in the family circle. Her eyes were swollen shut, her head the size of a basketball. Blood ran down her face, ears, and mouth. A catheter hung from her partially-shaven scalp, draining the excess fluid from the brain. IV bags dripped medicines into her body. The breathing machine rhythmically pumped air into her lungs.

I thought about Grandma's prayer. *Perfect? She's far from perfect.* I looked at Kendall and saw a hopeless situation. A meaningless death. An unexplainable tragedy.

I closed my eyes again, tuning back into Grandma's prayer. She continued. "Thank you, Lord. Her body is now perfect in Your presence."

Faith Has No Formula

Often in a crisis, we experience tension. On one hand, we believe God can intervene in our situation and do the impossible. On the other, we know God can also give us the supernatural ability to endure any tragedy and accept what happens. Both are expressions of faith. How then, should we respond?

In these puzzling dilemmas, we feel a tug-of-war between our emotions, our thinking and our faith. We don't know how to react. Rest assured—feeling this kind of tension is normal.

The apostle Paul faced this pressure in prison. His afflictions pulled him in two directions: glory in heaven and suffering on earth.

"If I am to go on living in this body, this will mean fruitful labor for me. Yet what shall I choose? I do not know, for I am torn between the two: I desire to depart and be with Christ, which is better by far; but it is more necessary for you that I remain in the body..." [13]

Paul believed God still had work for him to do—to serve and suffer for others. We must remember, there are no formulas when it comes to expressing faith. We rest our faith in a person, not a recipe. In these situations, knowing God's will helps us to know how to apply our faith. Once we grasp how God wants us to respond, the tension eases.

What truly matters in these situations? We focus our faith upon honoring Christ, not upon our desires or comfort.

"For me to live is Christ and to die is gain."[14]

Why Not Ask

When we don't know how to react in a certain situation, we can ask.

"If any of you lacks wisdom, you ask God, who gives generously to all without finding fault, and it will be given to you."[15]

God wants us to know His will. He has given us the Holy Spirit to guide, counsel and help us through the process. Why not take advantage of the resources we have been given? There's no need to worry, to be stressed or be perplexed about our crisis. We express faith by asking for assistance to know how to respond. Then we accept, believe and move forward. In Grandma's case, praying led her to accept Kendall's death.

The Multiple Faces of Faith

Faith expresses itself in many ways. Sometimes, we hope for miracles. We ask for deliverance, healing, and blessings. On other occasions, our faith transforms our circumstances into something greater. Believing changes our tragedies into triumph. Grandma saw what others couldn't: the unseen. By faith, Grandma saw her granddaughter's glorified body in heaven, the greatest miracle of all. Believing is seeing.

"Therefore, being always of good courage, and knowing that while we are at home in the body we are absent from the Lord—for we walk by faith, not by sight."[16]

Chapter 11

SEVEN THINGS DEATH
CANNOT TAKE AWAY

*Death cannot take away **eternal life**.*
God's promises heaven for those who believe.
*Death cannot take away **time** spent i*
nvesting in and influencing others.
*Death cannot take away your inner sense of **joy**.*
*Death cannot take away your **peace**,*
which surpasses all understanding.
*Death cannot take away your **faith** that*
God has a purpose for your suffering.
*Death cannot take away your **influence***
on the lives of other people.

*Death cannot take away your **hope**
and expectation of good things to come.*

*Where, O death, is your victory?
Where, O death, is your sting?*[17]

Chapter 12

OLD FRIENDS

Courage of Giving and Receiving Friendship

Old friends. Surgeons need them too. A surgeon's friends are the body's unchanging landmarks, easy to find and always there. Like the right renal vein, the duodenum and the renal arteries. When fixing a ruptured abdominal aortic aneurysm and blood wells up in the depths, your old friends show you the way. No need to panic. They are always there. These markers give a surgeon his bearings.

I walked into the intensive care unit to check on a patient who had survived a ruptured aneurysm. The operation was a success, but the patient was still sick. A ventilator pushed air into his lungs. Blood dripped out of the IVs into his veins. Tubes protruded out of every orifice.

I stood in the doorway and watched the nurse hang another bag of blood. "Has the family shown up?"

"Nope." She pushed buttons on the monitor and continued her work.

The patient had arrived unconscious before surgery. We were told he had no family. I needed to talk to someone about his condition. Peering down the hall, I watched an elderly man approach. Dressed in a suit and tie, he pushed a walker through the hallway. He gasped for breath, propped up his frail body, and beckoned me with a finger.

"Excuse me, young fella. Are you John's doctor?"

I nodded and walked over to him. "Yes, sir. We haven't been able to find any of his family. Are you a family member?"

His brown eyes sparkled. "Not exactly. My name is Robert. John and I go a way back." He smiled and gave a curious expression. "Well, how is he?"

"He's better than when he got here," I replied. "Can you tell me about John's medical problems?"

"We were in the Korean War together. John got shot in the leg and spent a month in a MASH hospital. Infection went into the bone." Robert snickered. "He's a tough guy. The army doctors thought he'd lose his leg, but he didn't."

The old man turned his walker around and sat in the little plastic seat. "About forty years ago, he jumped in front of a car in Ft. Worth. Broke his ribs and his collarbone. John seemed to settle down after that incident. The worst was when he got lung cancer about twenty years ago. The chemo almost killed him. Those were some tough times, but we made it through."

I smiled and listened to John's buddy recount his medical history. I realized Robert had experienced all those events firsthand. For fifty years, Robert had been there with his friend: encouraging, listening, counseling, comforting, and remembering. His detailed history revealed more than a hundred pages of electronic medical records could ever tell.

He continued, "He doesn't have any family left. Neither do I. We play dominoes together. We're the best forty-two team in town." He laughed. "We've got a big forty-two game next week. Do you think he'll be ready?"

While I listened to the veteran's stories about his friend, I realized what a blessing the two had been to each other. Both had received a special gift, one which many people never experience their entire lives: the bond of friendship.

Receiving Friendship

Often, we approach our circumstances with the "I got this" attitude. We think we can handle the pressure of being sick on our own. All we need is the Lord, we proclaim. No doubt—we are never alone in Christ. God is our source of help. But often, grace flows through others. Sometimes, we need to let someone minister to us. We receive God's supply through the deeds of a friend. We mustn't overlook God's helping hands. Accepting this expression of God's love requires vulnerability and humility.

Giving Friendship

Our hand of fellowship can be the vehicle by which God moves in someone else's circumstances. Are we available for others? Can we offer a quick phone call to encourage someone who is hurting? A text containing a scripture to ponder? An hour to sit, listen, and be with another in their time of need? Doing some chores to help someone recuperating? How about a game of dominoes with someone in need of company?

The Ultimate Friend

There are times when we suffer alone. Humanly speaking, we have no friends. All the crutches of our lives have been removed. This is the time in which we must recognize our greatest opportunity. We can look up to the throne of grace in our time of need. Our friend, Jesus, is there, interceding for us. We can look within, where the Holy Spirit abides.

The Comforter. The Counselor. The Helper. Because of the completed work of Christ, we are never alone. We can draw directly from the well of grace, receiving all that we need. This Old Friend never changes. He is always there.

"Greater love has no one than this: to lay down one's life for one's friends...I no longer call you servants...Instead, I have called you friends..."[18]

Chapter 13

EIGHT WAYS TO BE A FRIEND TO SOMEONE WHO'S HURTING

Visit them frequently.

Be there for them. Let them know when you are coming.

Take them to a medical appointment.

Park the car for them. Be a second set of ears in the doctor's office.

Keep an up to date health record for them.

Update their medication list. Organize their paperwork.

Do errands for them.

Mow the grass. Buy some groceries. Do some house chores.

Help pay the bills.

Keep the financial statements and bills up to date.

Help them schedule appointments, tests and procedures.

Endure the hassle and frustration so they won't have to.

Listen and pray.

Give them a safe place to unwind and to share their frustration

Encourage them often.

Send letters, notes and texts that remind them you're thinking about them.

Chapter 14

DUCT TAPE AND COLOSTOMY BAGS

Courage to Be Creative

M adge returned to the office one week after a difficult, though successful, surgery. We removed her rectal cancer but had to divert her intestines with a colostomy.

She returned earlier than expected. Her colostomy bag wasn't sticking to her skin. Her situation was getting messier by the minute.

She warned me before I examined her. "Don't laugh, Doctor. A girl's got to do what a girl's got to do."

She pulled up her shirt, grinned with a mischievous smile, and showed off her handiwork. "Well, what do you think?"

To hold her colostomy bag in place, Madge had covered her belly with duct tape.

"Doc, I had to do something. Either use duct tape or have poop spill everywhere."

I smiled, affirming her ingenuity. "Hey, what a clever idea. That's a lot cheaper than the stuff I use, and it works better. Can I borrow some of your tape for surgery tomorrow? It may come in handy."

"Sorry, that's the only roll I have. But it's on sale at the hardware store. Two for the price of one. I can even get it in camo colors."

I gave an approving smile. "The effluent will thicken up over time and will become more formed."

"What does effluent mean?" she asked.

"Your poop," I explained.

She squinted her eyes. "Oh, I see. Didn't know there were fancy words for poop. Well, do you have any better ideas about how to keep my *effluent* from spilling all over the place?"

I scratched my head. "Madge, let's not major on the minors. Heck, if it's working for you, maybe I should use duct tape for all my colostomy patients."

Madge used duct tape to express her individuality. Ingenious. Applying duct tape around her colostomy bag made sense. If I recommended another alternative, I could have hampered Madge's creativity and caused a mess. Trying to change her method would undermine her personality.

The Freedom to Be Yourself

God made *you* to be *you*. Everybody else has been taken. Let's remember to express our creative uniqueness during our adversity. Let's demonstrate His grace under pressure. God gave each of us a specific personality, passions, and experiences to show others His goodness. We mustn't be afraid to express our individuality. We are fearfully and wonderfully made to show others how God works in and through our difficulties.

Own Your Circumstances

There are some matters where choice is not an option. We must follow the protocol. Yet even in those situations, we can find opportunities to express our uniqueness. We shouldn't allow the things we cannot do to hinder our ability to do the things we *can* do.

All we need to do is be ourselves. We can express our uniqueness, creativity, and personality in our journey through suffering. We don't have to let the confines of our disease or our circumstances keep us from expressing God's goodness in our own unique way. Madge applied duct tape creatively, constructively, and liberally, and so should we.

"For you created my inmost being; you knit me together in my mother's womb. I praise you because I am fearfully and wonderfully made; your works are wonderful, I know that full well." [19]

Chapter 15

THE SPOON TWIRLER
Courage to Accept Our Struggles and Move Forward

T he recovery room nurse called about the girl who had her feeding tube removed earlier that morning.

"Angelica can go," I said over the phone.

"I can't let her go until you see this," the nurse replied. "You need to come and look at this."

I sighed over the phone. "What is it?"

"I can't tell you. Just get over here."

I scurried over to the discharge area, reviewing every step of her surgery. *What could have happened?*

Angelica was eight years old. She suffered from Phocomelia, a syndrome where the extremities do not develop properly in the womb. She was born without any hands. Her left arm appeared to be severed just below the elbow. Angelica's right arm was worse–a mangled stump of tissue. She had no hands, one elbow, and now, no feeding tube.

I thought of the insurmountable hurdles she and her family would face through her life. Angelica's *normal* would always be abnormal. The youngster's poor family had no resources to help her cope with her disability. Accomplishing the most ordinary daily activities would forever be a challenge.

When I arrived, the nurses were laughing, clapping, and cheering in Angelica's room. For some strange reason, the nurse closed the curtain behind her and stood like an emcee about to give an introduction.

The nurse motioned me to stop and then bowed. "Ladies and gentlemen."

She pulled back the curtain and the show began. Angelica smiled at the gathering crowd. A plastic spoon sat between her elbows. With her malformed arms, she dipped the spoon into the cup, grabbed a chunk of red ice and twirled the spoon. She rotated the spoon towards her mouth by torqueing her arms in a clockwise motion. Angelica swallowed the ice and rubbed her elbows in the opposite direction. The spoon twirled the other way, back to the original position. Again, she was ready to grab another chunk of ice.

The Spoon Twirler spun the spoon back and forth, repeating the process over and over, demonstrating poise, grace and precision. Like an Olympic figure skater, Angelica elegantly performed her task.

I gleaned a few pointers that day from a disfigured eight-year-old with Phocomelia.

Angelica Didn't Use Her Victim Card

We all have struggles—challenges that define our destiny. The outcome depends upon how we respond to our struggles. Angelica didn't see herself as disabled. Instead of becoming self-absorbed, Angelica viewed her obstacles through another set of lenses. She embraced her disability, accepted it, and made the best of her circumstances. Shouldn't we follow suit?

Like Angelica, we should learn to accept our challenges. When we take a God's-eye view of them, our tests become our testimony.

Angelica Worked Hard and Kept a Positive Attitude

Her inspiring ability didn't appear overnight. Like a well-orchestrated ballet, each step had been practiced hundreds if not thousands of times. For years, she and her parents practiced—over and over—each step of learning to feed herself. I wondered how many times Angelica spilled food in her lap, missed her mouth, and made a mess. I wanted to ask her mother how many times her daughter failed and wanted to quit. How many times had she become so discouraged that she dared not touch a spoon? Probably thousands. However, with determination, some help from her parents, and hard work, Angelica mastered the technique of feeding herself—without any hands.

Angelica Transformed Her Disability into a Demonstration

Like Angelica, our specific struggles, obstacles, and trials are part of God's plan for us to inspire others to fulfill their destiny. In our obstacles, we can find opportunities. Our problems can become possibilities. We can transform our mess into His message. What we consider our downfall, God may put on display, showing His goodness to others.

Let's think about our circumstances. God designed them for a grand purpose. He is strategic with our afflictions. Not only do our struggles define who we are, but they can also prove God's power is working through us. We should make the best of them.

"Dear friends, don't be surprised at the fiery trials you are going through, as if something strange were happening to you. Instead

be very glad—for these trials make you partakers with Christ in His suffering, so that you have the wonderful joy of seeing his glory when it is revealed to all the world." [20]

Problems
are not stop signs;
they are guidelines.

—Robert H. Schuller

Chapter 16

SAVED BY THE SMELL

Courage to Find Joy in Suffering

Medicine provides a unique window to peer into people's lives, especially in times of difficulty. Often, I am amazed at how some respond in adversity. Many suffer well. They fill their surroundings with the fragrance of Christ. One patient named Sid mastered the art of spreading a sweet-smelling aroma—along with some not too sweet odors.

Sid served as a missionary in Botswana, living out his dream. But at age fifty-four, everything changed. On a trip into the bush, a slithering Black Mamba bit Sid's leg. Then the venomous snake disappeared in the jungle, it's poison already at work in Sid's body. On the three-day trek back to civilization, Sid's organ systems shut down. He lost his kidney function by the time he arrived at the hospital, leaving him dependent on a dialysis machine.

Sid never returned to Africa. God put him on a new assignment. He ministered every Monday, Wednesday, and Friday at the dialysis clinic, sharing his faith. Over time, we became friends. I watched him deteriorate from chronic disease and performed several surgeries on his worn-out body.

I visited Sid in the hospital after he had a heart attack. I opened the door and peered in the room. Sid and his wife chuckled.

Curious, I walked in the room, "What's so funny, guys? Heart attacks are serious."

Sid giggled and looked over at his wife. "We were saved by the smell."

Intrigued by his comment, I stepped closer to his bedside. A foul-smelling odor hit my nostrils harder than a southpaw's left hook. I shook my head and came back to my senses. Still confused, I breathed through my mouth, trying to keep the stench from passing through my nose again. "What do you mean, Sid?" I asked. "It reeks in here. And why are you snickering about it?"

Sid roared with laughter, unable to catch his breath. I remembered his condition and looked at the squiggly lines on the heart monitor. I had never seen anyone die of laughter and didn't want Sid to be my first.

Ruby, his wife, chimed in. "Sid had to go to the bathroom and the nurse wouldn't let him out of the bed. She gave him a bedpan but forgot to come back."

Sid sighed. "As I was doing my duty, sitting on the bedpan, some friends stopped by. They stayed for almost half an hour. All the while, I'm sitting on the bedpan with my legs flexed. Before they could leave, a maintenance man came in to change the light bulb. By that time, the aroma had spread through the room. That guy set the record for a light bulb change. Doc, you should have seen the look on his face."

Ruby snickered. "That group left, and another group of church ladies came in. Those women were just as clueless. Fortunately, they didn't stay very long. By this point, the scent from my bedpan had spread out into the hallway."

Sid lifted his hand into the air and waved to heaven. "Hallelujah, saved by the smell."

I marveled. Although I encountered a hideous smell that day, I recognized another scent—the fragrant aroma of Christ. The odor from Sid's bodily functions was smothered by unexplainable spiritual joy.

Transforming Your Trials

Sid and Ruby endured many disappointments and setbacks as he battled heart disease. Their lives took several unexpected turns. Yet, by leaning into their faith, they transformed even the smelliest condition into a sweet spiritual aroma.

What about us? What do others smell when they see us suffer? Christians have been empowered to release a fragrant scent—even in their most challenging circumstances. The power that we've received gives us the ability to change the malodorous into the magnificent. So, let me ask you, are you emitting the aroma of Christ in your challenges?

Expressing the Fruit of the Spirit

Christians don't need to pray for patience in tough times. They already have it, they simply must tap into it. The Holy Spirit, present in the heart of every believer, provides a storehouse where patience can be found in their time of need. The same goes for the other characteristics of the Spirit—love, joy, peace, kindness, goodness, gentleness, and self-control.[21] The Spirit has already deposited these qualities into our lives. However, we must choose to yield, abide, and appropriate these resources.

Instead of asking for patience, we should try praying in this manner: "Lord, help me to draw upon the patience you have already given me.

Empower me to recognize and use what you have poured into my heart. Let it overflow."

During Sid's heart attack, he expressed joy. His joy flowed out of an abiding relationship with Christ and the ability to laugh at himself. Sid expressed a positive attitude when appearances were negative.

Instead of expelling a rank odor when life hits us hard, we're equipped to express a sweet aroma. This fragrance encourages and enlightens others. This sweetness oozes out when we tap into the power of the Spirit within us.

How Can I Express This Aroma?

By becoming a living sacrifice, we place ourselves on the altar of worship. We cannot offer anything to God that will gain His approval. If we've truly received Christ's offer of eternal life, then we're already accepted, because Jesus was sacrificed in our place. Because of what God has already done, we can offer our lives on the altar without fear. This expression of admiration, worship, and gratitude makes sense in the light of what He has done for us. Paul described his reasonable act of worship as a drink offering.[22]

In the Old Testament, drink offerings were poured on the altar along with the sacrifice for sins. When this mixture of oil and wine hit the hot coals, it evaporated into thin air. Nothing remained. The sacrifice was replaced with sweet fragrance. The refreshing scent filled the air and replaced every other smell in the room. Paul's drink offering should be our response to God.

The old us disappears when we pour out our lives. We are transformed, our smelly old habits, attitudes, and actions are replaced by a sweet odor pleasing to God, refreshing to others.

How are we smelling these days? What parts do we need to place upon the altar of worship? Our broken dreams? Unfulfilled expectations? Painful experiences? Challenging circumstances? An uncertain future?

Empty them on God's altar of worship and watch them burn away. All of them. They will vanish to be replaced by a refreshing bouquet of reasonable acts of service. Like Sid, we can pour everything on the altar of worship. When we do, we will experience a joy that cannot be taken away.

"But even if I am being poured out as a drink offering on the sacrifice and service of your faith, I am glad and rejoice with all of you." [23]

You don't earn grace,
and you don't deserve grace;
you simply receive it
as God's loving gift,
and then share it with others.

—Warren Wiersbe

Chapter 17

LIFE GIFT

Courage to Give

wo paramedics wheeled a young boy into the trauma room. One squeezed an air bag, blowing oxygen into his lungs. His partner pounded away on the boy's chest, counting compressions. "One. Two. Three. Four. Five." The patient's chest rose as the paramedic forced air into his body. Like two graceful dancers, they worked in unison: one breath for every five thrusts.

While they transferred him off the gurney, I assessed the monitor. A flat green line displayed on the screen, accompanied by a long, monotone beep. A nurse took over compressions while the paramedic caught his breath. "CPR for twenty minutes. No response. Pupils are fixed and dilated."

I examined his body. No pulse. No signs of life. Resigned, I walked towards the doorway. "He's gone. Call it."

One of the paramedics caught me at the door. "The boy and his older sister were playing on the apartment stairs—Cowboys and Indians." His face darkened. "She lassoed him with a rope, so he started a tug-o-war. He pulled the rope out of her hands and fell backwards off the stairs."

The paramedic paused, pointed to the boy and sighed. "The rope caught in the steps before he made it to the ground." The man's voice broke. "Witnesses heard a loud popping sound. He dangled there for several minutes." The paramedic stopped to swallow. "Sorry. We know he's gone, but we couldn't call it at the scene. The family wouldn't let us stop."

I examined the eight-year-old boy again, rechecked the leads to the monitor, and looked again at his neck. The impression left by the rope's choke-hold could still be seen under his chin, leaving a classic hangman's fracture. Nothing changed. His pulses were absent. I forgot I had already told the team to stop compressions. Thinking maybe no one had heard me, I raised my voice. "Call it. He's dead."

The nurse doing CPR ignored my order. She looked me in the eye and continued pushing on the boy's chest.

"Stop, Chelsea," I commanded. "He's gone."

Chelsea gave me a look of defiant desperation. "Come on. Let's give him another round of drugs."

"You're being driven by your emotions, not the facts. He's gone. There are no signs of life."

The nurse continued pumping on the boy's chest. A mutiny was brewing in the ER.

Health care workers—paramedics, nurses, and doctors—all share something in common. At the end of the day, when we lay our heads on our pillows, we think, worry, and dream about our patients. In those moments of silence, we ask ourselves the question, *did I do enough?*

Somethings haunt our minds for years. I realized this was one of those moments—one which would linger in the memory of everyone involved. No one wanted to live with any hint of regret.

I nodded my head. "Blast him with a jigger of epi, atropine, and calcium. Give him the kitchen sink—all at once."

I broke protocol, thinking one huge dose of medications would soothe everyone's conscience. This round of drugs was for the nurses, the family, and even myself, not for the patient.

But when the adrenaline hit his veins, something changed. The flat line on the monitor came alive with a normal heart rhythm. Within seconds, the boy's vital signs stabilized. I re-examined him. There were still no signs of neurologic activity. The nurses began cheering and with a self-satisfied tone, said, "I told you so."

But I didn't feel elated like everyone else. In my effort to comfort the minds of the health care team, I had created a more complex problem. The boy laying on the table was nothing more than a brain-dead vegetable with a beating heart.

I made my way to the waiting room alone, gathering my thoughts. The boy would now exist in a coma for many years, attached to machines. I'd stolen the family's chance for complete closure. They still suffered loss, but now had to live with the burdens of a brain-dead child.

When I opened the waiting room door, sounds of wailing and gnashing of teeth reverberated through my ears. I forced myself to enter, pushing my body forward through an invisible barrier. The boy's mother stretched herself out on the floor. Friends gathered, placing hands of comfort on her shoulder. She crawled on her knees, grabbed my scrubs, and looked into my eyes. "Don't tell me he's dead."

I explained the complicated situation we were now facing. "He's not physically dead. His heart is beating." I watched my words fall on deaf ears. "However, he has no signs of brain activity."

The mother let go of my scrubs and cried uncontrollably. I did our best to console the family. The chaplain came in and helped to shed light on the situation. "We don't always have explanations for these kinds of tragedies. But I believe somehow, good will come out of this."

Over several days, the family absorbed the truth, albeit in small doses. The child never woke up. His organs functioned, yet his brain demonstrated no activity. In time, the family made a heroic decision. As the chaplain suggested, they too wanted something good to come out of their tragedy. The family agreed to donate the boy's organs for transplantation.

With the help of Life Gift, a transplant service, the boy's organs were taken. Doctors gave the boy's heart to a six-year-old girl, whose own heart had failed. She received a new lease on life. They split his liver in half, donating each piece to two kids born with congenital liver disease. Two other children each received a kidney. The bone marrow was transplanted into a young child receiving chemotherapy for leukemia.

Via organ donations, several people received renewed life through his tragic death. Nothing could replace the beautiful boy who had been lost, but donation did provide closure and purpose for the family. Although an eight-year old child died, he passed life on to others. The gift of his being was multiplied.

The Great Exchange

Jesus gave the original *life gift*, offering the greatest exchange in human history. Through His death, we received life. Jesus' nature has been transplanted into us via the Holy Spirit abiding within. He gives us a new heart, a new mind, and new purpose.

Jesus' death was no accident. He loved, so He took the initiative to pass the Spirit of Lasting Life to us.

"He made him who knew no sin to be sin on our behalf, so that we could become the righteousness of God in Him." [24]

*For it is in giving
that we receive.*

—Francis of Assisi

Chapter 18

DADDY, THAT WASN'T SO BAD

Courage to See the Benefits of Adversity

S am screamed. His cheeks blushed and beads of sweat formed on his brow. Sam's father held the ten-year-old in his lap and whispered in his ear, "Sam, it's just a little ingrown toenail. You will feel better once the doctor removes that rotten thing."

Sam tried to break free from his father's grasp. Sam's dad couldn't convince him to be still.

I rubbed a topical gel over the toe, numbing the skin prior to injecting it with a needle.

"Look, Sam. That didn't hurt."

My reassuring words backfired. I gave the topical anesthetic extra time to settle in while drawing up the Novocain. When Sam saw the needle, he cranked up the volume, becoming more nervous and suspicious. His screaming made me long for a pair of earmuffs to drown out the deafening sound.

If only Sam understood just how good he has it. I turned away from the bawling kid, thinking of all the afflictions that *really* caused pain. Sam had no concept of *real* pain. His problem paled in comparison to the man with a flail chest I'd treated earlier that morning. His rib fractures evoked pain with every breath.

Sam didn't know of that man or his excruciating existence. Four people held the boy down while I injected Novocain into his big toe.

"Daddy, why are you letting them hurt me?" Sam said.

His dad tightened his grip. "Don't move. Be still."

While Dad steadied the boy's foot, I aimed my needle towards his wiggling toes.

Sam watched as the needle plunged into his flesh. "Aaaaaaaah." He screamed for a moment and then gave me a puzzled look. "I can't feel my toe." Sam exhaled. "Why can't I feel the needle?"

Dad loosened his stranglehold on Sam's hands. "Son, that's what the medicine does. It takes the pain away."

Sam laughed. The tension on his face disappeared.

His dad chuckled, stepped back and watched me prepare the instruments. "Son, why were you so scared?"

The boy smiled. "I didn't know what was going to happen. I thought you were going to hurt me."

I took a hemostat, shoved it underneath the toenail, and twisted the embedded portion of the nail out of its stronghold. Pus oozed out of the crevice where the nail had cemented itself. Sam never flinched.

"No wonder your toe hurt," his dad said, amazed at the size of the embedded nail.

"That was no big deal," Sam said. "I never felt a thing."

What We Fear and What We Need

A youngster's mind cannot comprehend the benefits of pain. Their thinking doesn't see beyond the present anguish. It hurts, and when it hurts, that's all that matters. We cannot rationalize, explain or excuse away pain in a child's brain. They live in the present.

Often, like children, we can't see past our present suffering. We can't fathom the healing pain often brings.

Sam didn't realize the needle was the remedy for his irritating toe. Like Sam, we can fail to recognize that the very things we fear are often the very things we need.

Like Sam, we let panic steal our peace. The *what if's* race through our minds.

What if it hurts?

What if the cancer comes back?

What if complications arise?

What if I'm worse?

What if I'm alone?

We know our anxiety is irrational, but our feelings overwhelm us. When we meditate on our fears, our faith wanes and our joy withers.

Replace Worry with Prayer

Instead of worrying, we can express our feelings, fears, and frustrations in prayer.

> *"Do not be anxious about anything, but in every situation, by prayer and petition, with thanksgiving, present your requests to God. And the peace of God, which transcends all understanding, will guard your hearts and your minds in Christ Jesus."* [25]

Fear Sees Only the Pain

Fear overwhelms our emotions, multiplies our irritation, and clouds our thinking. It focuses on the hurt without seeing its benefit. Worry fixates our minds on the imagined. We can't see past the pain of a needle-stick, knowing it will lead to healing.

Faith Sees the Product

Faith directs our thoughts to the benefits of our suffering. Faith sees the rewards, assuring us that our pain has purpose. Belief visualizes the future with confidence, looks beyond present difficulties, and focuses on the good which comes in the end.

Remember Who Is with Us

Rather than give our attention to the *what if's*, we should concentrate on *who's there* with us. Like Sam's dad, our Heavenly Father comes close in adversity. Often, we misinterpret His actions, thinking we are being punished.

Like Sam's dad, God gently reminds us of the purpose behind our pain. He never wastes our afflictions. He knows exactly how much we can bear and how long we need to endure it.

We can move forward with courage and confidence, knowing He is with us all the way.

"So do not fear, for I am with you; do not be dismayed, for I am your God. I will strengthen you and help you; I will uphold you with my righteous right hand." [26]

Fear. __False__ __Evidence__ __Appearing__ Real

Chapter 19

PROMISES TO OVERCOME FEAR

The LORD is my light and my salvation; Whom shall I fear? The LORD is the strength of my life; Of whom shall I be afraid? [27]

For I am the LORD, your God, who takes hold of your right hand and says to you, Do not fear; I will help you. [28]

For He Himself has said, "I will never leave you nor forsake you." So we may boldly say: "The LORD is my helper; I will not fear. What can man do to me?" [29]

For ye have not received the spirit of bondage again to fear; but ye have received the Spirit of adoption, whereby we cry, Abba, Father. [30]

And do not fear those who kill the body but cannot kill the soul. But rather fear Him who is able to destroy both soul and body in hell. [31]

So do not fear, for I am with you; do not be dismayed, for I am your God. I will strengthen you and help you; I will uphold you with my righteous right hand. [32]

Be strong and of good courage, do not fear nor be afraid of them; for the LORD your God, He is the One who goes with you. He will not leave you nor forsake you. [33]

I sought the Lord, and he answered me; he delivered me from all my fears. [34]

Chapter 20

ALL HAT, NO CATTLE

Courage to Leave Something Behind

H orace lived in a quaint country chateau on the outskirts of
Paris—a dairy farm in Paris, Texas, that is.

We have a saying in Texas to describe pretenders. *He's all hat
and no cattle.* A lot of people wear big fancy hats, mainly for show,
puffing themselves up for appearance, but Horace was the real deal. He
enjoyed the things that mattered: God, family, work, and other people.

I had patched his worn-out body together for several years. He
usually came to the office wearing his work clothes: faded overalls. His
boots, covered with dirt and cow manure, always left a trail behind him
on the waiting room floor. But on this day, things were different. Horace
returned for his post-surgery check-up dressed to the hilt. He wore a big
silver belt buckle and a fancy Stetson hat. Shocked by his dress, I hardly
recognized the old rancher.

"Well, look at you, Horace. Where's your overalls?"

Horace smiled. "Well, I slicked up for you today. I think you did a decent job with that knife of yours."

I nodded, grateful for the clean boots on his feet today. "Horace, where'd you get that fancy hat?"

"Doc, you wouldn't believe me if I told you. I won this hat and a saddle in the Panhandle, back in the day. 'My Eighter from Decatur.' Riding that bull was the longest eight seconds of my life."

I knew Horace tended to stretch the truth—just a little. "Horace are you pulling my leg?"

He looked out the window, trying to change the subject.

"I went to town this morning and someone offered me a hundred dollars for this old hat."

Horace took the Stetson off his head, held it in his hands, and stared at it. I could tell he was pondering something. He sighed, and with a resolved expression, handed the hat to me. "Try it on."

The white felt hat had a ring of dried sweat at the bottom. A thin leather belt wrapped the base and a small silver buckle shined on the front. Classy but weathered. Like Horace, I knew the old hat had a yarn or two it could tell. That Stetson expressed Horace's personality.

"There's no other hat like this one in the world. Go ahead, try it on."

The hat fit perfectly on my head. I took it off and handed it back to Horace. At first, he hesitated. Then he raised his hands to stop me.

"Nope. It's yours to keep. Wear it with pride."

And I did. I still wear that Stetson, today.

Like Horace, I learned to pass the hat around. His gift wasn't mine to keep anyway. Horace's hat became a conversation piece and a source of cheer for many people. People loved wearing Horace's hat. A sick kid. A fellow health care worker. Someone who needed a laugh. A purple-haired widow with a fancy hairdo. Horace's hat put some smiles on some faces, made people feel special and lifted a lot of heavy hearts.

I cherish Horace's old ten-gallon more than any degree, award, or accomplishment. He gave me his hat, not because I deserved it, and certainly not because I earned it. Giving his hat was Horace's way of showing goodwill. Horace loved, so Horace gave. He was the kind of man who would give you the hat on his head.

Love Gives

What's your hat? What do you have worth giving to someone?

Your life experiences?

Words of encouragement?

Perspectives on circumstances?

Laughter amid tears?

Thoughtful acts of kindness?

How will you express God's love to others? You'll never know how your generosity can influence someone until you give your hat away.

We often think of the grandiose things we leave behind. But what about the small things, priceless little pieces of our person, little reminders of God's grace, forgiveness, and goodness? Our hat may be a word of affirmation, a nod of acceptance, or a thoughtful appreciation. When we pass it on to others, the bearer of our hat may wear it proudly for years to come.

The tiny treasures we give may leave a greater impression than any material thing we leave behind. We shouldn't forget to spread little acts of kindness. Our significance lies not in what we take but in what we give. What will our loved ones remember about us when we're gone?

"Let us not become weary in doing good, for at the proper time, we will reap a harvest if we do not give up. Therefore, as we have opportunity, let us do good to all people, especially to those who belong to the family of believers." [35]

Do all the good you can.
By all the means you can.
In all the ways you can.
In all the places you can.
To all the people you can.
As long as you ever can.

—John Wesley

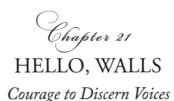

HELLO, WALLS

Courage to Discern Voices

I stood in the emergency room hallway and peered into Mildred's room. In a defiant voice, she said, "Nope. I can't do that. You're crazy."

Her eyes moved to and fro, swinging like a pendulum. The nurse handed me her chart and pushed me into the exam room. "She's schizophrenic. Swallowed a fork today at the funny farm. You'll need to fish it out of her stomach."

I held my breath and walked into the room. Mildred's eyes stopped their see-sawing. "It tasted good. Can it stay in?" Mildred looked back at the wall and started talking again. "Hmmm. I never thought of that. What a good idea."

I looked towards the wall, searching for Mildred's friend. There were no people, only an X-ray displaying a fork sitting sideways in Mildred's stomach.

Mildred smiled at the empty wall and shook her finger. "You got me into this."

Later that afternoon, we put her to sleep. I passed a scope down her mouth and into her stomach. I lassoed the fork, pulled it through her esophagus and sent Mildred back to the mental institution.

The next week, I received a phone call from her psychiatrist. "Well Doc, she did it again. This time she ingested some batteries. Will acid rot a hole in her stomach?"

We transferred Mildred to the hospital, removed the batteries and shipped her back home. Three days later, the emergency room called. This time, she had scarfed down some razor blades.

Mildred bounced back and forth from the hospital several times during the next month. Frustrated by the ordeal, I began to question my own sanity. Who was crazier: me or Mildred? I remembered the adage, *Insanity is doing the same thing over and over, expecting a different outcome.*

I knew removing the razor blades wouldn't fix Mildred's real problem. She would come back. She needed more than an adjustment of her medications. Mildred needed to confront the voices speaking into her head.

I tried some reverse psychology on my schizophrenic patient. This time, I sat down at Mildred's bedside, held her hand and began talking to the voices. "You're not really Mildred's friend. You're giving her bad advice. Mildred's my buddy. Friends don't tell friends to do things that hurt them."

Mildred, shocked to have someone converse with her voices, shook her head. Anger filled her face. She squinted her eyes and scowled at the wall. "He's right. You don't really care about me. Leave me alone."

Mildred and I scolded the empty wall, rebuked her voices and rejected their suggestions. After five minutes, I looked into the hallway. A crowd of nurses and hospital personnel stood outside the door, eavesdropping on our conversation.

Then, an emergency room doctor peered into the room. He told the nurse, "Give Mildred a shot of Haldol. And put that doctor in a straight-jacket."

After removing her razorblades, I never saw Mildred again. I don't know if my creative treatment worked or if they transferred her to another institution. Either way, Mildred taught me some things about listening to those voices that sometimes talk in our heads.

The Lying Voices

You don't have to suffer with schizophrenia to hear voices. Sometimes, we all hear those utterances persuading us to do things we know will tear up our insides. They often tell us to ingest harmful things.

When we follow their suggestions and swallow the goods, we experience pain. With regret, we know we shouldn't have listened. Like Mildred, we get caught in a vicious cycle.

Sometimes, the voices whisper half-truths into our minds. They twist our thinking. They convince us to do things we know we shouldn't. They tell us…

Just try it one time. It won't hurt.
You're alone. No one will know.
Everybody else is doing it. How can it be wrong?

Sometimes the voices attack our identity and our purpose.

You're a nobody. You don't measure up. You'll never be good enough.
You're not important and you don't make a difference.
God could never forgive you for what you have done.

Other times, the voices deceive us about spiritual things.

God doesn't care about you.
You're suffering has no purpose.
Your life doesn't matter that much spiritually, give up on God.
Don't bother praying; God doesn't listen to your prayers.
God's promises aren't true; stop believing them.

Replace the Lies

We need to learn to distinguish the source of those voices. Whatever untruths the utterances suggest, you can choose to ignore them. Don't listen to their lies. Like Madge, reject them and replace them with reality.

Victorious thinking comes by letting truth speak into our situations. When we fill our minds with God's principles, we leave no room for fuzzy thinking. How many times has God encouraged his people to listen to His voice?

> *"His sheep follow him because they know his voice. But they will never follow a stranger; in fact, they will run away from him because they do not recognize a stranger's voice."* [36]

We can listen to the voice of God inside us, coming through the Holy Spirit. If you have received Christ, then God's strength, wisdom and discernment live within. God doesn't want us to be confused about what we hear. Ask the Spirit to enlighten your mind and learn to discern when He speaks. Listen and fill your mind with God's certainties. The gentle voice of the Master tells us,

> *You are significant, because I love you.*
> *I have created you for a unique purpose.*
> *I died for you. You are already forgiven, accepted and loved. Walk in it.*

Everything you need, I have already supplied. Don't search for substitutes.
I control your circumstances and I am sovereignly good.
In Me, you are good enough. You are complete, adequate and equipped.
If you will come to Me, I will bear your burdens. My cross is easy,
and My burden is light.
Apart from Me, you can do nothing. Abide in Me.

Learn from Mildred and her crazy doctor. Ask God for discernment. When those voices squawk lies into your mind, confront them with truth. Battle them with help of the Spirit. Receive the sound mind and the strong heart God has promised.

Everything you need to conquer your enemies has already been provided to you. You have the authority to choose. Simply listen and obey the voice of God.

"Whether you turn to the right or to the left, your ears will hear a voice behind you, saying, 'This is the way; walk in it.'" [37]

Grace grows best in winter.

—Charles Spurgeon

Chapter 22

THE VIRTUAL PRISON

The Courage to Live in Freedom

A man named Fred came in for an office visit. He complained of several skin growths on his body.

"They itch, Doctor," he said. "And I notice them constantly."

I examined his hands. Two trivial skin lesions protruded from the top of his hand. They were discolored but had all the features of a benign growth.

"I would leave them alone. They look like seborrheic keratosis. The more you age, the more they will appear."

"Doctor, I looked it up on the internet. Web MD says they're malignant melanomas."

"Yes," I responded. "Melanoma is one possibility. But look at the lesions. SKs look like old bubble gum stuck onto your skin. Google seborrheic keratosis and you'll see a perfect description of your lesions."

The man's wife interjected, "What if you're wrong?"

While I did my best to reassure them, our discussion escalated into an argument. Nothing I said could ease my patient's fear. Convinced he had skin cancer, the man and his wife persisted.

"If you don't take them out, I'll go somewhere else."

I hid my aggravation, but something stopped me from showing him the door. "Okay, if the lesions are bothering you, then we'll bother them. We'll schedule you for an excision next week in the office."

"No," he said. "Put me to sleep. I don't want to feel anything."

Frustrated, I felt He was wasting my time. People with real problems—cancer, infections, and chronic wounds—were waiting to be seen.

Now we had to have another discussion: weighing the risks of a general anesthetic for a procedure typically performed in the office.

On the day of his surgery, Fred and his wife brought their condescending attitude with them to the hospital. Nothing pleased them. They nitpicked everything. Fred griped to the front desk lady about the paperwork. He questioned the wording on the consent forms. He complained when the nurse placed the IV in his arm. He fussed because his procedure had to be delayed for a more urgent one.

The nurse taking care of Fred asked me, "Where did you get this guy? We have bent over backwards trying to please him. Everything we do is wrong."

Finally, the time for Fred's surgery arrived. I went to the bedside to mark the lesions. He lay on the gurney in his hospital gown. I looked down at his feet. Shackled around his ankle was a black circular ring with a flashing red light.

"What's that?" I asked.

"I'm ashamed to tell you," Fred whispered. "I'm being monitored. They want to know where I am at all times. I'm a convicted child molester. I had a relationship with a minor. We met on an Internet chat site and arranged a time to get together. When I showed, they got me. The whole thing was a set-up."

Embarrassed, his wife chimed in, "Everything we do is under surveillance. The authorities will not allow him to drive in front of schools. We must take alternative routes. Even the simple, everyday things are complicated."

Fred bowed his head in shame. "My probation officer shows up at the house when we least expect it. They call us on the phone at weird hours, just to make sure we are where we say we are. We live under constant scrutiny. If I screw up, or fail to report my whereabouts, I could be thrown in jail." A tear filled my patient's eye. "I live in a virtual prison. I'm sorry for what I've done. I've learned my lesson, but I'll never be free from my past mistakes."

How often do we assume things about people before we completely understand their situation?

After hearing his story, I understood Fred's eccentric behavior. When someone lives under constant scrutiny and knows a minor slip results in major consequences, they tend to respond back in the same fashion. How can someone understand grace when they only experience condemnation?

The Natural Response

When no one gives you the benefit of the doubt, you return the favor. Like Fred and his wife, you become skeptical, judgmental, and unforgiving. You question everyone's motive. You innately treat people in the same fashion you have been treated. An eye for an eye and a tooth for a tooth becomes your natural response.

Christians shouldn't be surprised when unbelievers act in this manner. They do what they do because that is their nature. Good for good. Evil for evil. The unbeliever often responds in the way they have been conditioned.

However, the born-again should react differently. Instead of rising above our circumstances, forgiving and forgetting, and living through the Spirit, too many continue living in bondage. Our shackles have been removed, but we keep living as we've been conditioned, trapped in a virtual prison.

Freedom: Seeing Yourself Through God's Eyes

We can embrace freedom and live in liberty or we can choose to live in bondage. The defeated, imprisoned mindset that judges and condemns others, and even ourselves, holds us captive. We see God as a traffic cop. We believe He hides and waits for a mess up, then He punishes us for our shortcomings.

Jesus did not come to condemn. We were condemned already. He came to earth, then died and rose again, to set us free.

What is your virtual prison? Can you identify the chains that bind you, hindering your freedom in Christ?

What attitudes, habits, and mindsets shackle your ability to experience the abundant life you are promised?

Freedom Begins with Desperation

We begin by seeing ourselves as we truly are: defeated sinners. We must acknowledge our inadequacy. We can never measure up to God's expectations. Without God, we can do nothing, but don't let these truths discourage you.

Many believers stop there and live in defeat. Although they have been released from their shackles, they still cling to their prison bars. They are free—at least in God's eyes—but they never experience the abundant life Christ promised. Why?

Freedom Cannot Be Attained by Your Own Strength

God never planned for us to live the Christian life on our own. The thought never crossed God's mind for His children to exist in their own strength. God never asked us to manufacture goodness, faithfulness, integrity, and love on our own. So, let's stop trying.

We cannot muster enough dedication, discipline, and determination to please God without assistance. Let's stop beating ourselves over the head, trying to live up to God's standard of perfection alone. We cannot release ourselves from our virtual prisons. God has a better way.

Accept the Way God Sees You

Based on the finished work of Christ, we are accepted. Jesus took our place and suffered judgment, so we could experience His grace. We must accept our acceptance. If we have placed our faith in Jesus, God sees us through a distinct set of lenses. Because of the completed work of Christ, what we must do has already been transformed into done.

We are forgiven. The penalty of our sin has been removed and is no longer our master.

We are adequate because of Christ's sufficiency.

We are secure. Nothing can separate us from the love of Christ.

We are competent through His awesome power working in our lives.

We are whole, not in ourselves, but in the completeness of the One who died for us.

Living the Exchanged Life

We don't have to be like Fred, living in bondage. We can receive God's unconditional acceptance and let abundance flow through our lives.

Apart from Him we can do nothing, but through Him we can do all things. The key to living in freedom comes by letting Christ live through our lives. We must abide in His presence, depend upon His strength, and draw upon His resources. When we live in this manner, we live in freedom. We are free.

> *"It is for freedom that Christ has set us free. Stand firm, then, and do not let yourselves be burdened again by a yoke of slavery."* [38]

There is one thing
God cannot do.
He cannot see your sin if it
has been covered by Jesus.

Chapter 23

MENDING FENCES

Courage to Face the Facts, Forgive and Be Free

S unday morning, six a.m.

I received my daily wake-up call from the emergency room. While I dressed, I counted my blessings. *At least they didn't call at 2 a.m., the time the patient arrived.*

I rushed through the ER hall, hoping to make it to Sunday services. I avoided the front desk, bypassed the nurses and headed straight for the patient's room.

He was sleeping it off when I arrived. I leaned over the patient's blood-caked body and shook the bed.

"What's your name?"

He opened his eyes, grabbed his head and exhaled. Like a dragon emitting fire, his breath reeked of alcohol. Startled by his response and the smell, I stepped back from the bed.

"Can you tell me what happened last night?"

"The name is Elton. Elton Jones."

His voice, slurred by the alcohol and a broken jaw, sounded like someone with a dozen marshmallows stuffed in his mouth.

"I was on my way to Sunday School, minding my own business, when suddenly this plate glass window attacked me."

I nodded, wondering why I even asked in the first place.

"Elton, that window must have a strong left hook. I've never seen a window break someone's jaw."

Elton smiled with the half of his face that wasn't broken. "Can I go home?"

"Not hardly. We need to fix your broken mandible."

I walked out of the room, preparing to finish the paperwork. Mandy, one of the ER nurses, motioned me to the side. She wore an embarrassed and shame-filled expression.

"Is he going to be okay?"

I was taken aback by Mandy's question. Seasoned ER nurses don't express much emotion for beat-up drunks. They are an everyday occurrence in the emergency room.

"What's up, Mandy? Do you know the guy in trauma room three?"

"He's my father." Mandy bowed her head. Elton had embarrassed his daughter again. This time, he did it in the presence of her peers.

I tried to look into Mandy's face, but her eyes were fixed on the floor. "This is not the first time this has happened, is it?"

She shook her head.

"When was the last time you saw your dad?"

She looked up at me, her face turning red. "About two years ago. He was in a car wreck." Angry tears filled Mandy's eyes. She turned away for a moment, looked back into her father's room, and gathered her composure. "He abandoned us when I was a kid."

I thought about Mandy, her dad, and their fractured relationship. His jaw would be an easy fix, but the broken bond with his daughter went beyond my expertise. Healing emotional wounds are complicated, messy and slow. I looked through the curtain at Elton. The consequences of his choices damaged more than himself. Mandy had suffered deep wounds. Bruised feelings. Broken promises. Failed expectations.

I turned around to talk to Mandy, but she had vanished, already off to take care of another patient and attend to another problem. I finished my paperwork, gave final instructions and made a beeline for the door. If I hurried, I could catch the last part of Sunday school.

I walked out the emergency room door and nodded to medical personnel wheeling another patient inside on a stretcher. I sighed in relief. The patient on the gurney didn't look like he had a surgical problem.

I walked to the car, thinking about Elton and Mandy. My mother's face flashed into my mind. She had died of lung cancer several years before. I thought about the things I should have said and the time I had wasted. Then it hit me: I knew my work in the ER wasn't finished. I did an about face and walked back inside. Sunday school would have to wait.

I found Mandy clicking keys on a computer. "Mandy, I lost my mother three years ago. I have some regrets. There are things I should have said but never had the courage to tell her. Don't make the same mistakes I did."

Mandy gave me a blank stare.

"You can't change your past, and you can't change your father. But you can change your future. For your sake, go and mend some fences with your dad."

I never did find out if Mandy and her dad ever got things right.

Take Advantage of the Moment

Doors of opportunity can close quickly. Our circumstances may lead to an occasion for mending a broken relationship, if we don't wait too long to act.

It's important to remember that we don't have to be overwhelmed with a forgiving feeling before we forgive. Our emotions can deceive us. Reconciliation is best based on facts and decisive acts. Not only did Jesus take our place and forgive our transgressions, He took the initiative. He did not wait for us to get it all together before deciding to die for our sins. He reached out to reconcile our relationship.

If you are a follower of Christ, you must follow His example. You need to make the first step to forgive, even when it is painful. Since Christ initiated our reconciliation, we must offer the same sacrificial acts to others.

Moving beyond Feelings

Most people base their actions upon their own feelings. Negative emotions surface—anger, resentment, anxiety, shame—and irritate us like a wound that won't heal. Each time the affliction is touched, we re-experience the pain. Wounds fester and never heal until they are addressed, hindering our progress forward.

Healing Begins with You

We cannot change the past, but we can change our future with God's help. We cannot change others, but we can forgive them. Spiritual, emotional, and psychological healing begins with us. We often miss the point of the parable about the unforgiving servant.[39]

The servant, who had been forgiven much by the king's generosity, failed to forgive a much smaller debt. Consequently, the king placed him in the dungeon to be tormented until the servant paid back everything he owed. If we have been forgiven by Christ and fail to forgive others, we place ourselves in a position of ongoing emotional torment.

Your Offenders Can't Release You

Forgiveness is not about others; *it's about us.* We don't have to be imprisoned in our self-made dungeon. We don't have to be tormented by damaged emotions, shameful regrets, or a guilty conscience. As a physician, I've seen how short life is. We can't wait for those who have offended us to come and free us. They can't anyway. They don't have the power to do so. We must release ourselves to experience freedom.

The unforgiving servant's imprisonment was conditional. He could only be released if or when he paid what he owed back to the king.

Like the servant, we can't repay our debts either.

Use Your Get-Out-of-Jail-Free Card

No one is capable of paying back the balance owed to God for our sins. So, let's stop trying. Instead of wasting our efforts, let's accept the payment offered for our release. Agree with the King's conditions and live by His rules. Forgive those who have offended you. Liberate yourself from your self-imposed shackles.

Regardless of how others respond, God promises to set us free from our prison when we obey his command to forgive. We can't allow our offender's choices to keep us in chains. We will never heal, we will never fully experience transformation, and we will never live up to our potential until we realize that forgiving others is more about us than them.

When we forgive others, God frees us from our dungeons. Grace steps in and heals. In His goodness, our heavenly Father will break the chains that keep us locked up.

"And his master was angry, and delivered him to the torturers, until he should pay all that was due him. So My heavenly Father will do to you if each of you, from his heart, does not forgive his brother's trespasses." [40]

If you can forgive the person you were, accept the person you are, and believe the person you will become, you are headed for joy.

—Barbara Johnson

Chapter 24

THE DEMONSTRATION

Courage to Show Others God's Love

F lorence came to the office with dysphagia. Instead of sitting on the exam table, she stood by the door, holding a plastic bag in one hand and a cup of coffee in the other.

"I can't swallow," she said flatly.

I asked the standard medical questions, working through the list of possibilities. "Do you have more problems swallowing liquids, or solids?

"Doctor," said Flo, "I told you, I throw up everything."

"Has this difficulty been progressive over time or a sudden onset?"

Flo sighed. "Over about a year."

"Does anything make it better or worse?"

Flo tapped her fingers on the chair, her voice growing in defiance. "No. *Nothing* makes it better. *Nothing* makes it worse."

My patient's frustration grew with each question. Ignoring her emotions, I continued the interrogation. I searched her chart, looking for studies on the computer.

"Do you ever regurgitate undigested food? Does it go down all the way?"

Exasperated, Flo tapped me on the shoulder. She squinted her blue eyes, grabbed her cup of coffee, and gulped it down.

I watched her peculiar behavior, wondering what she was up to.

Flo began to fidget. "Yep. I swallow and then it comes back up later."

The expression on Flo's face changed. She looked like a volcano ready to explode.

Flo grabbed my arm, pointed to her chest and gagged. Seeing that she was about to spew, I pulled away. But Flo wouldn't let go of my arm. The volcano erupted. At the last moment, she opened the plastic bag and regurgitated. Then she wiped her mouth with her forearm, released me, and then handed me a full sack of vomit.

Speechless, I gagged and held the bag of up-chucked coffee away from my face.

"This is what happens when I swallow." She pointed her bony finger towards her chest. "Fix it."

I got the message. Her demonstration helped me understand her malady in seconds. Up close and personal. Case settled. No further questions.

Showing Trumps Telling

Demonstrations possess power. They express more than a million words can describe. Ask any vacuum cleaner salesman or infomercial guru. They know how to sell their goods. If they can show their product's effectiveness and utility, then few words are needed.

Dr. Luke, who wrote half of the Bible's New Testament, reminds us about God's powerful demonstrations. Luke wrote to tell us "about all that Jesus began to *do* and teach."[41] The Word, God's ultimate expression of love, dwelt among us, displaying His compassion, authority, and goodness to mankind. Jesus confirmed His words by His actions.

Jesus' life spoke volumes, but His death revealed His unconditional willingness to go the distance.

God didn't just tell us how much He loved us. He demonstrated His love by accepting a hideous death, exposing Himself to shame, and then showing His power through suffering.

What about us? How are we demonstrating God's power in our afflictions? Whether we live, die, or suffer, our anguish provides an opportunity to follow in His footsteps. We must never underestimate the impact of giving small expressions of kindness. Our acts of service, especially when we're suffering, speak more than they ever could when things are going well. People take notice when we respond in an unnatural way to our painful circumstances

Invite God to Use Your Circumstances

No matter what we're going through, God's already centered in our situations, ready to show His power and faithfulness. Our affliction can become His greatest platform. However, we must choose to let God transform our troubles. We must ask ourselves, am I using my afflictions to model God's nature to others?

Brainstorm

How can we demonstrate His goodness and adequacy? We can be creative.

We could secretly pay for a stranger's meal at a restaurant.

We could visit a nursing home and spend time with those in drastic need of attention.

We could stop and pay attention to that person who often annoys us.

What about the people God places in our path daily? The lonely neighbor next door. The lady next in line for chemotherapy. The attendant who wheels us down for X-rays. How about the home health or hospice nurse? If we're sick, we have numerous opportunities to bless others with a listening ear and by being a friend who will pray.

We can bring a little bit of heaven into someone's circumstances. The possibilities are endless. There are millions of ways we can show God's love to others. Just ask Flo's doctor. Nothing gets our point across like a demonstration.

"But God demonstrates His own love toward us, in that while we were yet sinners, Christ died for us." [42]

*A good example
is far better
than a good precept.*

—Dwight L. Moody

Chapter 25

THREE WORDS

Courage to Tell

T he dictionary defines purgatory as a place of mental anguish, a transition zone existing between two places, a realm where no one desires to stay.

I know purgatory exists, because I lived there for three months in 1996. I survived the Fondren-Brown Intensive Care Unit in Houston, Texas, on coffee and adrenaline instead of sleep. I lived like a zombie, caring for the sickest people on the planet, biding my time until moving on to bigger and better things.

Like purgatory, the patients in Fondren-Brown existed somewhere in between life and death. Most survived. Others didn't. Still others, like Arnie, lingered in purgatory for months—too sick to be transferred out, yet too healthy to graduate into eternity.

Arnie's seventy-year-old lungs weren't strong enough for him to breathe on his own. He underwent experimental surgery to improve his lung capacity. The operation was a success, but Arnie survived on a ventilator.

I addressed the urgent problems in the ICU every day, the acute problems of sicker patients taking priority over Arnie's chronic ones. Over time, Arnie picked up on my lack of attention. One day when I came into his room, he grabbed my scrubs.

I leaned over his bedside. "Arnie, what's wrong?"

The tracheal tube, attached to the breathing machine, kept him from talking. He mimed words I couldn't understand. I didn't have time to guess. I reassured him with a pat on his foot and moved on to the next patient.

From that moment, Arnie schemed to get my attention. The next morning when I rushed through on rounds, he disconnected himself from the ventilator tube. He placed his finger over the hole in his trachea and tried to talk.

"Hey," he rasped.

For a moment, time stopped. Arnie got everyone's attention. Monitors beeped out of control. Nurses came running. Arnie's lungs quickly tuckered out.

I reattached him to the breathing machine. "Arnie, are you out of your mind? You could've killed yourself."

Arnie responded with a mischievous smile. He showed no concern about the risk he had taken.

Arnie's odd ritual continued for a couple of weeks. He would pull the breathing tube out of his neck and speak one or two words before shortness of breath depleted him. The nurses noticed a pattern. He only did this when I came around.

One day, one of the nurses stopped me in the hallway. "I think Arnie has something important he wants to tell you. If you would talk to him, maybe he would stop detaching himself from the ventilator."

That afternoon, I finally had an opportunity to talk with him. I sat at his bedside. "Arnie, is there something you want to tell me?"

He took a deep breath, like a diver about to plunge into the abyss. He removed the breathing tube and placed his finger over the hole in his neck. He whispered, "Jesus loves you." His lips turned blue. He gasped for air. Exhausted, Arnie couldn't say anything else.

Arnie's three words took *my* breath away. I had heard that message, millions of time. But this time, the words sank deeply into my soul.

I reattached his tubes, silenced the alarms and smiled. "Thank you, Arnie. I really needed to hear that today. You'll never know how much this means to me."

I watched Arnie's vital signs normalize. His lips turned pink again. His face expressed relief, celebration, and victory. Mission accomplished. His blue eyes sparkled, and a knowing grin crept across his face.

My beeper went off and our window of time together closed. I rushed out of Arnie's room pondering those three words, thinking about the risk he took to deliver the message.

Later, I finished my shift, still pondering the message. Arnie had made his three words count. With intention, he risked his life to show God's love to a sleep-deprived surgeon in-training.

Returning to the ICU the following morning, I learned Arnie had passed away. I had no doubt he had fulfilled his purpose. He demonstrated God's faithfulness, goodness, and love until his life came to an end.

Think about It

Arnie left a lasting impression on me. He didn't dwell on his suffering, pain, or confinement. He chose to live above his circumstances and transformed his greatest adversity into his greatest message. He took a great risk, just to remind me I am loved and not alone. I am forever grateful for his efforts.

If we only had breath for three words, what would they be? Someone desperately needs to hear our message in the way that only we can give it. Will we recognize our suffering as an opportunity to draw people's attention to God's power? Will we take risks so others can experience God's love? Arnie did. Will you?

"My message and my preaching were not with wise and persuasive words, but with a demonstration of the Spirit's power, so that your faith might not rest on human wisdom but on God's power." [43]

*He who loves with purity
considers not the gift of the lover,
but the love of the giver.*

—Thomas àKempis

Chapter 26

HOW *NOT* TO DELIVER A BABY

Courage to Keep Perspective

I will never forget my first day of call in medical school. Neither will my patient.

It was Easter Sunday, 1993, in the obstetrical ward of Ben Taub General Hospital, Houston, Texas. I had never delivered a baby, and she had never had one.

I could tell the Spanish-speaking mother felt both excitement and anxiety about the birth. So did I, but I didn't let on. In medical school, you fake it until you make it. You *pretend* you know things that you really don't. You *pretend* to do things you can't, until—eventually—you learn to do them.

After hours of labor, the time came for my patient to deliver the goods. Anxiously, I pushed the woman to the delivery room. The mother lay on her side on the gurney, moaning more intensely with each contraction.

"Aaaaaaayeeeeeee!" She cried out prayers in Spanish, trying to push her baby out before we reached the birthing room.

I shouted the commands my superiors taught me. "No *empuje*! No *empuje*!" Don't push. "*Inspire profundo.*" Breathe deeply. My command to stop fell on deaf ears. She kept pushing. The baby kept coming. I pushed the bed faster down the mile-long hallway, wondering if we would make it to the room before the baby delivered.

After what seemed an eternity, we arrived and moved the mother onto the table. Her crying changed tones. Her groans turned into screams. "Aaaayeeee! Aaaayeee! Aaaaayee!" I put her in the stirrups while the nurse prepped the back table. The baby moved quickly down the pike. I sat on the delivery stool, wondering what to do next. Fortunately, the seasoned nurse standing behind me knew exactly what steps to take. This was not *her* first rodeo. She yawned, and then shouted at the top of her lungs: "Empuje! Empuje!"

I followed suit and let out a battery of *empujes.*

While the mother screamed, I sat on the stool, preparing to deliver my first baby. I reviewed the instructions my superiors gave me, step by step: how to place my hands and catch the baby, how to suction out the lungs and how to clamp the umbilical cord. I remembered the most important thing they told me, "Whatever else happens, *don't fumble the football.*"

My heart raced with anticipation. This wasn't a dream. All those years of biochemistry were finally paying off. I was delivering my first infant, like a *real* doctor. The mother screamed out something in Spanish and pushed. When she did, a large volume of bloody fluid splattered on the floor. While blood spattered on my shoes, the baby's head appeared.

I turned and looked back at the nurse behind me. "She's crowning."

The nurse disregarded my comment and continued to scream, "Empuje! Empuje!" I looked around the room, embracing the moment. Suddenly, a wave of panic pulsed through my body like an electric current. I had never delivered a baby and my supervisors were absent. A series of *what ifs* entered my mind.

What if something goes wrong?

What if the baby's head is too big?

The nurse, oblivious to my fear, kept telling the mother to push. Voices of doubt raced through my head. *You're only a medical student. You have never seen a delivery before. You are a pretender.*

The mother yelled again, but the pattern changed. Gone were the long-winded wails. She let out a series of staccato shouts. Like bullets out of a machine gun, she cried. *"Aye, aye, aye, aye, aye."* The baby's head protruded out of the canal.

I felt the room growing warmer. I looked up at the mother's face, now covered in sweat. My scrubs were drenched in blood. I felt a strange, woozy sensation creep through my body. The room began to spin. My vision dimmed. While the baby moved forward, I saw myself moving backwards through a dark tunnel, traveling farther away from a bright light. Suddenly, the light vanished. Everything went black.

I woke up on a gurney in the recovery room. My head throbbed with a dull pain. I sat up, looked around and yelled, *"Empuje!"* The mother, resting in the bed beside me, gave me a puzzled look. Then she cried and mumbled in Spanish.

The delivery nurse walked in between us. "Lay down. You passed out. She believes her baby is sick or disfigured. She thinks you passed out because of what you saw. With all the commotion in the delivery room, she never got to see the baby before we sent him to the pediatrician."

Easter morning, 1993, was the most embarrassing day of my life. I have never lived it down. I didn't become an obstetrician; however, I did finish medical school. And I learned some principles the hard way, which helped me to persevere in tough times.

Confidence

Sometimes, we want to quit. We make mistakes. We feel isolated, fearful and discouraged by our troubles. In these times, we need to learn perseverance. Our confidence doesn't lie in our ingenuity, abilities or experience, nor in self-reliance. Our firm assurance rests in God.

God doesn't place us in circumstances we can't handle without His help. There are no accidents. We are placed in situations for reasons. God promises to be with us, to equip us for our challenges and to reward us when we pursue His will.

> *"So do not throw away your confidence; It will be richly rewarded.*
> *You need to persevere, so that when you have done the will of God,*
> *you will receive what he has promised."* [44]

Confiding builds confidence. Are we spending time meditating on God's promises and confessing our troubles? Are we praying for God's help and guidance? It's okay to ask for strength, insight and wisdom. The more we confide in God, the greater our spiritual grit and perseverance.

> *"For the Spirit God gave us does not make us timid, but gives us*
> *power, love and self-discipline."* [45]

Don't Go Alone

That Easter morning, I realized too late that I was in over my head. With a little preparation, I could have asked a resident to stop by and look over my shoulder. It might have helped me to see someone else do a couple of deliveries before I launched out on my own. We have a saying in training, "See one, do one, teach one." The effective Christian life follows the same example.

The book of Hebrews reminds us to stay connected. Those *let us* passages[46] remind us not to journey alone. We need other believers. Often, we feel isolated because we haven't taken the initiative to connect with someone else. We need people to watch and learn from; we need people to pick us up if we fall. Eventually, we need others we can teach.

Learn to Laugh

We need to stop taking ourselves too seriously. No one dies of laughter, but plenty of people die in need of it. We need to stop taking ourselves too seriously. When was the last time you laughed at yourself? Laughing promotes emotional, physical and psychological health. As a doctor, I've seen its healing power.

Laughter…

Releases our endorphins and lowers our stress hormones.
Improves our mood and changes our outlook on our problems.
Boosts our immune system and improves our health.
Relaxes tired muscles and increases our resilience.
Lowers blood pressure and improves heart health.
Eases anxiety, diffuses anger and diminishes stress.

Persevere with confidence, gather friends, and fill your lives with laughter. The Bible says it best:

"A cheerful heart is good medicine, but a crushed spirit dries up the bones."[47]

Chapter 27

THOUGHTS ON LAUGHTER

"Laugh at yourself first, before anyone else can."
—Elsa Maxwell

"Against the assault of laughter, nothing can stand."
—Mark Twain

"Humor is a prelude to faith and
laughter is the beginning of prayer."
—Reinhold Niebuhr

"Laughter is the sun that drives winter from the human face."
—Victor Hugo

"A good laugh is a mighty good thing,
a rather too scarce a good thing."
—Herman Melville

"Always laugh when you can. It is cheap medicine."
—Lord Byron

"He who laughs, lasts!"
—Mary Pettibone Poole

"A good laugh heals a lot of hurts."
—Madeleine L'Engle

Chapter 28

THE MARRIAGE COUNSELOR

Courage in Loss

I hurried into the exam room, behind schedule, trying to catch up. Charlie, a recovering stroke victim, sat on the table. He'd come to the office to have his feeding tube removed.

"How are you?" I asked, reaching out for a handshake.

With great effort, he reciprocated. Like a robot, Charlie stretched out his right hand, advancing it in rigid, slow movements. "G…go…goo…good," he replied.

The stroke also affected his speech. Unable to express his thoughts clearly, his wife, Sue, filled in the blanks for him. She interjected. "Charlie's always been the strong, silent type. I do most of the talking anyway."

I pulled out the tube with a strong heave. Charlie gasped. Then his shock quickly turned into celebration. Removing the feeding tube meant better days ahead for him and Sue. The couple enjoyed a small victory in their lengthy battle for Charlie's recovery.

My quick fix gave us a little time to visit. The more we talked, the more I recognized the shared mannerisms, personalities, and behavior between husband and wife. In their years together, the two had become one. Apart from death, they were truly inseparable.

"How long have you two been married?" I asked.

"Sixty-three years," replied Sue. "Wanna know the secret?"

I nodded, curious to hear their secret.

She smiled towards Charlie. "Be strong enough to bend. Show respect in front of your kids. An always, *always* kiss her goodbye before you leave for work. If you do this every day, you'll have a happy marriage."

"That's a good formula," I responded, heading for the door.

"Thanks for seeing Charlie," she said, "and one more thing."

I released the doorknob to turn and listen.

"When it's broke, you fix it. When things break, your generation wants to throw them away. Televisions. Appliances. Cars. Even marriages. But not our generation. In our day, when something broke down, you fixed it. Work on the little things every day. If you don't, they become big things over time."

Leaving their room, I realized something. I had learned more from ten seconds with Sue than at most weekend marriage conferences.

A year passed. One morning, Sue scheduled an urgent follow-up.

I entered the room expecting to see Charlie, but he wasn't there. His wife sat in the corner alone, exhausted and afraid.

"Charlie had another stroke this morning. He's in the ICU. Things don't look good. I came here because I knew you would know what to do."

I looked into her face and searched for an answer, but I couldn't find one.

"How can I live without him, after all we've been through together? We were just getting our lives back. Why now?"

Later that afternoon, I stopped by the intensive care unit only to find that Charlie had just passed on. I wondered, *What do you say to someone who's just lost her lifelong partner?* Fortunately, I didn't have to say anything. Sue chimed in, "I know I can face this. God has promised to always be with me. He never lets me go. Not even death can separate me from Jesus."

Getting through

Losing someone we love deeply makes us feel intense pain and we need to give ourselves permission to grieve. Anger, loneliness and confusion overwhelm our emotions, but they cannot separate us from the love of God. In our loved one's absence, we should remind ourselves of God's presence. Sue assured herself of God's promise to be with her in times of loss. For the faithful, we are never alone.

> *"Be strong and courageous. Do not be afraid or terrified because of them, for the Lord your God goes with you; he will never leave you nor forsake you."* [48]

In Jesus Christ, believers experience the fulfillment of His Word. We can face tragedy, loss, and affliction because God promises to never leave us. Nothing can separate us from the Holy Spirit, the comforter who comes alongside, living within, strengthening us in our trials.

Our Unbreakable Union

For the Christian, the source of our strength and courage comes from our union with Christ's Spirit. We can do all things through Christ because the Spirit empowers, enlightens, and assists us in our trials. Nothing can separate us from the abiding love of God. Death, life, present circumstances, past failures, an uncertain future—even cancer—can't separate us from Christ.

Always with You

Sue and Charlie were an earthly example of the believer's sacred bond—the marriage between God and us—that no man, circumstance, or transgression can destroy. Nothing can separate us from God's unconditional love. Take courage. God is with us. *Always.*

"Never will I leave you, never will I forsake you." [49]

***True love stories
never have endings.***
—Richard Bach

Chapter 29

DIAGNOSE THEN PRESCRIBE

Courage to Understand

G wen's stomach gurgled like a commode flush. She struggled to suppress her desire to vomit. "I'm so nauseated."

She grabbed her husband, who was trying to keep his distance, and covered her brow with a washcloth. "Rick, I don't know if my diarrhea is a side effect of the chemotherapy, or if it's cancer.

Gwen burped, retched and then hurled green fluid on their white carpet. "Call the doctor," she croaked.

Rick ran to the kitchen and called the oncologist's office, working through the maze of prerecorded options given for the directory. Punching in the code for Gwen's doctor, he got a message. *"If you're calling after hours with a problem, please go to the nearest emergency room."* Rick hurried back to tell his wife.

Gwen bowed her head, wiped sweat off her face and looked at the mess on the floor. "Oh honey, I forgot. Dr. Shaw doesn't go to the hospital anymore."

Rick scooped Gwen up and rushed her to the emergency room. When they arrived, Gwen was assessed quickly. Then Gwen and Rick were left alone while they waited. And waited. And waited.

After four hours, two nurses walked by during shift changes.

Gwen said, "Nurse, I thought this was a 'no wait' ER?"

The nurse rotating off her shift gave Gwen an irritated look. "You don't have to wait to be seen, but you still have to wait for your test results."

The nurse coming on smiled at Gwen. "I'm Thelma. I'll see what I can do."

Gwen and Rick could see through the window as Thelma sat down at a desk and tapped keys on a computer. The doctor who'd seen Gwen earlier was also in the room.

Rick noted the doctor's computer screen. "I can't believe it. He's on Facebook."

Gwen held her tummy. "Doesn't anyone care anymore?"

Tests had been ordered. Medications had been given, but the couple still waited for the physician to communicate with them. Rick paced the room. His face reddened. "I'm about to blow a gasket."

A woman wearing a white coat down to her knees entered the room. She obviously overheard Rick's complaints.

"I'm Jean, the nurse practitioner. You have a small bowel obstruction. We are calling a surgeon in to see you."

Gwen looked puzzled. "I have diarrhea. Wouldn't a blockage in my intestines slow down my bowel movements?"

Rick interjected. "You haven't even examined my wife. What is a small bowel obstruction and how do you know she has one?"

"We saw it on the CAT scan. You're the third one today." She yawned and looked down the hallway. She appeared distracted and disinterested. "Be patient with us; we have several people who are a whole lot sicker than you."

"Do you know she is receiving chemotherapy for ovarian cancer?" asked Rick.

Jean gave an unconvincing nod. Before she had time to explain herself, a nurse peered in the door.

"You're needed in the cardiac room. Heart attack."

"Sorry, I have to go. The surgeon will be down soon." Then Jean turned and left.

Gwen and Rick looked at each other in dismay.

"She didn't even ask about your medicines, your chemo treatments, or your symptoms."

Gwen added, "How does she know I have a bowel obstruction? She didn't even touch me. I thought we came to the emergency room to see a doctor?"

Failure to Diagnose

How would you feel if someone prescribed a treatment before making the right diagnosis? Like Gwen and Rick, we resent people who hurt us instead of help us, especially when we are suffering.

Some things have been lost in our new age of "click the box" medicine: listening and hearing, the skill of asking questions, the power of the human touch. For generations, medicine depended upon clinicians who built relationships, sat at the bedside, and performed thorough examinations. Today, the art of medicine has been replaced with a computer screen. Technology has replaced relationship. First, we prescribe, then we diagnose. It's all backwards.

But before we point our finger at the broken medical system, let's look at the three other digits facing back in our direction. For the sake of brevity, let's concentrate on our relationships.

First, Listen

If we're not careful, we can slip into distracted attitudes when dealing with others. We prescribe before we diagnose. We fail to listen, forgetting to understand another's needs. We assume things before we obtain all the facts. Sometimes, we exhibit this mindset with the ones we love the most. Parents, do you look at your child's problems through your own lenses without considering their point of view? Spouses, what works for you should work for your partner. Right?

Listening involves hard work. When we take the time to fully understand the needs of others and to see things from another point of view, amazing things happen. Hearing and understanding helps make the correct diagnosis. We need to listen to understand.

Put Others before Yourself

We prescribe what works for us, without taking time to hear both sides. Haste makes waste and hurts more than helps. We alienate those who try to assist. We say things we wish we hadn't. We jump to conclusions about our loved ones' motives and attitudes. We prescribe the wrong treatment, because we've made the wrong diagnosis. Like Gwen and Rick, others feel ignored, unvalued, and unloved when we approach them in this manner.

Wouldn't our relationships be richer, stronger, and deeper if we learned to show our care? What if we asked more questions, rather than making statements? What if we strived to understand?

Suffering brings bittersweet opportunities. We should use our time wisely while we have it. We can restore broken relationships and mend some fences, by listening and diagnosing properly. Asking first before jumping to conclusions can prevent a lot of pain.

> *"Do nothing out of selfish ambition or vain conceit. Rather, in humility value others above yourselves, not looking to your own interests but each of you to the interests of the others."* [50]

Chapter 30

PHYSICIAN, HEAL YOURSELF

Courage to Ask and Receive Healing

A stinging pain pulsed through my back, down my leg, and into my big toe. I left the hospital and hobbled to the clinic, unable to feel my left foot.

On the way, the nurse from the recovery room called my cell phone. "How many more units of blood do you want to give this patient?"

I sighed. "Give two more units of packed red blood cells."

I thought about the ruptured spleen I had just removed. The patient weighed four hundred pounds. My back pain began when I bent over and pulled out his spleen. A crazy thought entered my mind. *Can a doctor sue a patient if they have injured him?*

When I arrived at my office, a patient walked out the door. Disgruntled, he saw me approaching. With sarcasm, he asked, "How was the golf game?"

I bit my lower lip. Explaining where I'd spent my last hour wouldn't make him stay. I slipped through the back door and rushed into the first exam room. A child screamed when I entered, her face red, her eyes closed. Upon examination, I discovered a swollen, festering abscess covered her backside.

I glanced at the mother, looking faint in her chair. Her face appeared flushed and her hands clutched the seat. After instructing my nurse, I drew up some local anesthetic and said to the fidgeting mother, "We need to drain this abscess."

Four people held the kid still while I injected Novocain into the shrieking girl's leg. Bending over put me into an awkward position. While the girl's discomfort disappeared, the searing pain traveling down my back and leg returned. I needed to schedule an appointment with a doctor, if only I knew a good one. I finished numbing the girl and tried to straighten up, but my back locked in place.

I left the room, giving the anesthetic time to settle in. I walked next door, bent over, struggling with the numbness in my leg. But I had to push through. The lady in the next room was waiting for her colonoscopy results. Last week, I found cancer in her colon. To complicate the issue, she had cirrhosis. I reminded myself of a surgical proverb: *Cirrhosis plus surgery equals death*. But what happens when you add cancer to the equation?

My issues paled in comparison to hers. I grabbed the doorknob and looked to heaven, whispering, "Lord, how much more can I endure today?"

Elsa sat on the table accompanied by her pastor.

"Elsa, how's it going?"

She watched me hobble into the room and replied, "I'm doing a lot better than you are."

I winced, straightened my back, and took Elsa's hand. "I'm sorry to tell you this, but you have colon cancer."

After a moment of silence, she replied, "I knew it. I shouldn't have waited so long to have a colonoscopy."

Her head sagged. Tears fell down her face.

Elsa's pastor placed his hand on her shoulder, providing much-needed comfort.

I went through her options. "Your real risk lies not in the surgery, but in how your liver will respond to the stress." I straightened my back and grimaced. "The liver helps the body heal. Your cirrhosis will slow down the healing process and make you more prone to bleed."

The pastor interjected, "Doctor, we know you are a good surgeon, but you cannot heal. Can I pray for the both of you?"

We both nodded. The pastor placed one arm on Elsa and the other around my back. "Let's ask the Great Physician for help." He voiced a simple prayer. "Heal Elsa's liver and let the surgery be successful." He paused for a moment and then continued, "Lord, this doctor is doing your work; please heal his back."

I thanked the pastor, scheduled Elsa's surgery, and returned to the first room. The child's pain had left her. She slept on the table. When I bent over to drain the abscess, I noticed something incredible—the flexibility in my back had improved.

After draining the abscess, I moved on to the next room. Over the next hour, my back pain subsided more. Progressively through the afternoon, my back symptoms receded, my flexibility increased, and the numbness in my leg disappeared. Driving home after the long day, I felt the presence of God's love like never before.

Coincidence? I doubt it. I believe God healed my back. A week later, He also healed Elsa, surprisingly, but through a different means. God healed Elsa with a scalpel. Her surgery went well and her liver held up through the stress, refuting the surgical proverb.

God Heals in Many Ways

I can't explain how God did it—in either case. Considering her risk factors, Elsa's recovery was more miraculous than mine. Sometimes, there are no earthly explanations. Jesus didn't have a formula when it came to healing. With Jesus, every encounter, each need and every person was unique, but asking in faith was required. That level of trust is still needed today.

Are we willing to let go of our preconceived notions and give God room to intervene in our behalf? I believe we have not because we fail to ask with the right heart.

Asking with the Right Motive

The power in the pastor's prayer was not *what* he asked for, but *why* he asked. The pastor asked for healing to help both Elsa and I honor God with our lives.

God honors the prayer that honors Him. Our petitions typically revolve around relieving our discomfort, intervening in our circumstances, or cleaning up our mess. We throw up selfish, self-centered prayers. We ask amiss, petitioning God to intervene in *our* situation. Instead, we need to pray for things that enhance His reputation and give Him credit, no matter the final outcome.

Let's Pray

We can ask God to show us His will in our circumstances. We can ask for insight into what to pray for. He has no intention of keeping us in the dark. We can pray for healing. Pray for our doctor. Pray for our friends. Pray for difficult things. Pray. Pray. Pray. When we pray, the impossible happens.

"Therefore confess your sins to each other and pray for each other so that you may be healed. The prayer of a righteous person is powerful and effective." [51]

"Faith is taking the first step, even when you don't see the whole staircase."

—Martin Luther King, Jr.

Chapter 31

THING ONE AND THING TWO

Courage to Give and Receive

Medicine can be your friend, but it can also be your foe. The *art* of the craft comes from distinguishing between the two.

Shelly had survived a multitude of operations and endured every conceivable complication. She had suffered much in the hands of many surgeons. For five years, I treated Shelly for episodes of small bowel obstructions. My goal was to do no harm and keep her out of the operating room. I'll never forget the day when she introduced me to her two best friends: Thing One and Thing Two.

"I'm too busy to be sick," Shelly said, laying down on the exam room table, pointing to her stomach. Her belly was swollen to the size of a beach ball. "I've got another case of gas bloat. Can you fix me?"

I inspected her abdomen, a checkerboard of scars. There were too many to count. One in particular intrigued me, however. I pointed to the upside-down, T-shaped mark on her midriff. "Tell me about this surgery."

"Oh, that was a botched abdominoplasty. They took the muscle out of my tummy to replace my breast when I had cancer. After three operations, that muscle finally died. Now, I'm a flat-chested sixty-year-old woman with a beer belly."

I percussed her swollen abdomen with my fingers. A hollow drum-like sound resonated through her midriff.

She laughed. "Why don't you stick a needle in my belly and let the air out?"

"Shelly, I think that's a great idea."

Reaching into a drawer, I grabbed the biggest needle I could find, putting it in the full view of Shelly. I gave her a mischievous smile. "Be still; this won't hurt me a bit."

Her eyes widened with panic. She looked at the horse needle and put her hands over her stomach. "Let's think about this first."

I had called her bluff. "Shelly, if I operate on you, I will likely kill you."

I put the needle back in the drawer. "You see, surgery begets surgery."

Shelly nodded. "I resemble that statement."

I continued her examination and noticed two fist-sized knots on either side of her abdomen. She winced when I touched them.

"What are these?" I asked.

"Oh, that's Thing One and Thing Two. They've been there for years, mesh from botched hernia surgeries."

She gave a half-serious, half-sarcastic smile. "At least they match. I'm symmetrical. Flat chested with two thing-a-ma-jiggers coming out of my swollen belly. But no one can ever say I'm not equally proportioned."

Thing One: Focusing on Others

Over the next several years, Shelly endured multiple bowel obstructions without having to undergo surgery. She seldom ever ate a solid meal and blended her food to help digest nutrients.

During this period, I learned how Shelly kept going. With each visit, she shared about people she was helping. Shelly donated her time to various ministries, helping people worse off than her. She assisted those suffering with cancer, drove others to doctor's appointments, and raised money for those who couldn't afford medicine. She adopted an abandoned teenager named Julie suffering with advanced thyroid cancer. Julie had no place to stay and no one to care for her, except for Shelly. Shelly opened her home, her pocketbook and her heart, helping raise money for Julie's medical expenses.

Shelly's secret to persevering, in spite of her own intense pain and suffering, grew from her devotion to serve others.

When we give our time, treasure, and talents to others, a miracle occurs. We realize we are not alone, and our burdens don't feel as crushing—our own suffering diminishes. We don't have time to throw pity parties. We learn God's precious secret of living by giving.

Thing Two: Receiving by Giving

This truth defies our natural way of thinking. When we look at our overwhelming needs, we believe we have nothing to give. But the opposite is true. In God's economy, those who give of themselves receive *more* in return. When we pour our lives into others, God steps in. He ministers to us, meeting our needs as we serve others.

God sent the prophet Elijah—hungry, exhausted, and persecuted—to a starving, discouraged widow[52]. Both learned about God's provision. When the widow poured out the oil and dished out the flour, God provided for her needs as well as the prophet's. Yet the provision didn't begin until the starving widow prioritized Elijah's needs first. After she served food to the prophet, God's generosity was released.

If we are honest with ourselves, sometimes we feel like the widow. Our needs overwhelm us. How can we give anything? We feel destitute.

We receive by taking the initiative. When we give of ourselves first, we draw on God's generous supply. We will find that our cup runs over from a supernatural source.

Elijah and the widow were two beggars who helped each other find food. Their relationship defied explanation. Both parties received from the Lord. Both benefited from the other's sharing. Both the prophet and pagan were blessed, giving, receiving, and learning of God's generosity.

How can we meet our needs?

If we are lonely, we should reach out to someone who is lonely.

When our finances are exhausted, we should give generously.

When we're discouraged, we should strengthen someone else's faith.

In so doing, our needs will be met.

We would do well to follow Shelly's example. Remember Thing One and Thing Two? Shelly did not allow her contrary intestines to keep her from doing God's business. She concentrated on others. In the process of giving what she could, God met Shelly's needs.

The same principle will work for us. When we learn to give—not out of our abundance, but of our poverty—God shows up. Shelly's maladies became her platform, used to demonstrate God's generosity.

"And God is able to bless you abundantly, so that in all things, at all times, having all you need, you will abound in every good work."[53]

When all our hopes are gone,
it's best our hands keep toiling on
for others' sake:
for strength to bear is found in duty done;
and he is best indeed who learns to make
the joy of others cure his own heartache.[54]

—George Matheson

God's promises are medicine for the broken heart. Let Him comfort you. And, after he has comforted you, try to share that comfort with somebody else. It will do both of you good.

—Warren Wiersbe

Chapter 32

THE WANDERER

Courage to Be Thankful

T he emergency room doctor didn't tell me the whole story when he called me to admit Lester to the hospital.

He had been admitted with a snakebite, but his diagnosis didn't explain his bizarre constellation of symptoms. I leaned over the hospital bed and reached out for a handshake. "Hello, sir."

Lester didn't respond. He lay in his bed looking like a zombie. With an absent stare, he gazed at the ceiling.

I introduced myself to the family, pulled back the bed sheets and examined the snake bite. Two symmetrical puncture wounds located above his ankle protruded from the skin. The fang marks were scabbed over, the leg was covered with bruises. I could tell the bite occurred several days earlier, but Lester's snake bite was only part of his problem. The soles of both feet were covered with blisters, cuts, and scratches. Small red dots covered his skin, erupting with small pus-filled blisters.

The family paced the floor around Lester's bed, waiting to hear my opinion. I picked up on their emotional intensity and tried to speak some reassuring words.

"Must have been a copperhead. Sometimes, they bite, but they don't envenom." I smiled at the daughter. "And that's good. No venom in the tissues means no surgery."

My attempts at comforting the family failed. His three children continued to hover over him, like buzzards circling over a dead body. The oldest looked angry. The middle child seemed detached, but the youngest daughter wore an expression of guilt.

The longer I examined Lester, the more I felt like a crime scene investigator on a TV program. How could a demented old man scuff up his feet, suffer a snake bite, and be painted with bizarre red dots on his skin?

I scratched my head. "Does he live at home?"

The guilty-looking daughter spoke up. "Yes, I take care of him. He has Alzheimer's."

I gave her a puzzled look and then reexamined Lester. The old man's case sounded like something from a Sherlock Holmes story.

"Tell me what happened."

His daughter's voice quivered. "I was only gone for five minutes. He was sleeping in his chair. I went to the store and thought I could get back in time." She paused long enough for a regretful tear to run down her face. "When I came back, he was gone. I ran through the house but couldn't find him. I searched out the yard, but he wasn't there. I walked down the road and yelled out his name. In no time, he had vanished."

Intrigued, I urged her on. "Then what happened?"

"We called the sheriff. They searched everywhere. Even brought out a helicopter."

I nodded. "So, he wandered off. Where did he go?"

"They found him three days later almost ten miles away. He wandered barefoot through the woods. A farmer found him in a run-down barn. He fell asleep in an ant bed."

We Forget What We Should Remember

Forgetfulness allows us to wander off into all kinds of mischief.

Sometimes, like Lester, we wander spiritually. We find ourselves lost and alone with no recollection of how we got there. Our misadventure begins when we don't call to mind the ways God has shown up in the past. Instead of trusting in the certainty of His promises, we meander, putting ourselves in harm's way, leaving our safe place. It leads to danger.

Think about what happened when Israel suffered from a case of spiritual amnesia. Several days after crossing the Red Sea, they faced a new challenge: no water. Thirsty and hungry, they grumbled, complained and wanted to turn back. They forgot how God provided for their safety, parted the waters and defeated their enemies at just the right time. Instead of drawing on their Red Sea miracle and marveling over God's provision in an impossible situation, they strayed.

Are we forgetting the things we should remember? Do we remember all the times in our past where God pulled us through, provided for our needs and did the impossible? Let's stop mumbling. Let's quit dwelling on the uncertainties of our present situations. Let's recall the times when God showed up and parted the waters for us. Write them down and focus on how God has delivered. When we recall His promises, we're less likely to meander off.

We Remember What We Should Forget

Another mistake of human nature comes by reminiscing about the past, thinking the good ole days were better than they were. The Israelites did it to.

Craving water, Israel began to dream about the juicy melons of Egypt. Their current circumstances made them wish for the days gone by, but they failed to recall in their current crisis that their past was worse. Those sweet delicacies of Egypt came with a price: slavery. Making bricks without straw. The stinging whip of their taskmasters. The good-ole-days weren't so wonderful.

In our present afflictions, we shouldn't sugar-coat our yesterdays. We must forget those things that lie behind and keep moving forward. We shouldn't live in the past—successes or failures. We can trust God to take care of our present needs, knowing our future is in His hands.

Be Thankful

How do we concentrate our minds on the things we should? By nurturing gratitude. When we recite the times God has pulled us through, we cultivate our faith in the present. Nothing helps clear our thinking like appreciating God's goodness.

Thank God, He knows better than we do about our present challenges.
Thank God, He has our back and works our troubles for our good and for His purposes.
Thank God, we have a future hope.
Thank God, our past failures can be redefined as we move forward.
Thank God, our needs—not always our wants—will be provided.
Thank God for His promises, which we can draw on in challenging times.
Thank God, we are forgiven. Our past sins are forgotten.
Thank God, our suffering has meaning.
Thank God, He is with us guiding, strengthening and protecting.
Thank God, He is above all things and in Him all things hold together.

Nothing confuses our minds more than complaining and grumbling. The reverse is true about thankfulness. Nothing keeps us from wandering like gratitude. Let's count our blessings.

"Give thanks in all circumstances for this is God's will for you in Christ Jesus." [55]

Yes, let's give thanks for all things,
foras it has been well said,
"Our disappointments are
but His appointments."

—Arthur Pink

Chapter 33

YOU CAN PULL ALL YOU WANT

Courage to Handle Criticism

S tacy is one of my heroes. She's tough. Filled with sass, spunk, and
sarcasm, she uses her short frame to get patients moving after
surgery. She is a physical therapist who suffers with alopecia. She
has no hair. Yet, Stacy views her adversity from a unique perspective—
she never has a *bad hair day*.

One Saturday, I walked out of a patient's room during rounds and
heard a horrific scream. "Leave me alone! You're killing me!"

The hallway was empty. No nurses in sight. Suddenly, another shout
resonated down the lonely hospital corridor. "Help! Police!"

At first, I blew it off and continued my rounds, expecting someone
else to handle the situation. I had a tight schedule—no time to get
involved. But the scream occurred again, echoing down the hallway.

I heard the yelling come from the room two doors down. I realized I couldn't expect someone else to help. *What if someone is truly being assaulted?* I reminded myself of all the bad situations I had experienced in hospitals. Murders. Fights. Suicides. With caution, I moved towards the door, entered the room, and anticipated the worst.

But I did not witness an aggravated assault. Instead, I saw Stacy gently pulling an elderly lady out of bed. The frightened woman scowled at the physical therapist. "Quit, you pervert. Leave me alone!"

Stacy turned to me and grinned. "Well, don't just stand there, dude. Help me get her out of bed."

With reluctance, I stepped in and helped my friend sit her patient on the edge of the bed.

Stacy's red wig sat cockeyed on her head from tussling with the old lady. Frustrated, she sighed, adjusted it and stared at the bewildered senior. "You're almost there. Now grab hold of this walker."

In one final act of defiance, the patient gritted her teeth. "If you don't let go of me, I'm going to pull out your hair."

Stacy laughed, bowed her head and let the belligerent patient grab her wig. "Here ya go. You can pull all you want."

The lady tugged with all her might but met no resistance. Startled at first, the elderly woman didn't know what to think. Bewildered, she gazed at Stacy's bald head and then at the wig in her hands, believing she had pulled the hair straight off Stacy's head. The dumbfounded woman held the red wig in her hand. She had nothing more to say. The screaming instantly stopped.

I laughed and watched Stacy carry on with her shiny, bald scalp exposed. Game over. Stacy one. Patient zero.

Stacy carried on with her therapy. Only now , the elderly woman complied, stood up and grabbed the walker, with Stacy instructing her all the way. The fight had ended.

Imperturbability

The fifty-cent word, *imperturbability*, describes a posture of being steadfast and consistent during adversity. One displays imperturbability when they carry on, undisturbed by the surrounding chaos, and when they are immovable in purpose. They display a will focused on moving forward, despite the obstacles. Like Stacy, we need to adopt this attitude when facing criticism. Toughness without, tenderness within.

Sometimes when we're sick, living with a chronic illness, or suffering through a difficult trial, our defenses weaken. Trivial things that normally wouldn't bother us affect us a great deal. Under these conditions, loved ones offer well-meaning but poorly-timed words. Friends are absent when we need them most. We often interpret people's attempts to help in the wrong way.

Like pouring alcohol in an open wound, the pain sometimes multiplies. In those seasons of suffering, our heightened sensitivity makes us feel vulnerable, inadequate, and lonely. Remember the example of a bald physical therapist. Let people pull at our hair all they want. Display imperturbability.

Neutralize Your Enemies

When we confess our true condition, there's nothing else for others to say. Let them criticize us with their lengthy list of insults. Shock them by beating them to it, instead of defensively trying to deny. We need to remind ourselves that without Christ, we have no rights, we deserve condemnation, and we are unworthy. It is only because of him we are free.

A Heavenly Left Hook

Once we've quieted the fault-finders, we shouldn't stop there. Hit them with a greater truth, a left hook they will never see coming.

We can remind our critics of how God sees his people. Because of His grace, none of us receives what we truly deserve. Others may pull at our hair all day long, but because of God's unmerited favor towards us, it won't hurt a bit. Through God's eyes, we are perfect, redeemed, forgiven, and filled with purpose.

We must stay the course. Remember Stacy's wild wig trick?

Defuse your enemies and move forward with confidence. Fulfil your purpose. Finish the task. Laugh with our enemies. You can even agree with them. Let your hair down and expose your baldness. By doing this, you will heap coals of grace upon their heads. And who knows? Your greatest critics may become your friends.

"Do not repay anyone evil for evil. Be careful to do what is right in the eyes of everyone. If it is possible, as far as it depends on you, live at peace with everyone." [56]

*There is only one way
to avoid criticism:
Do nothing,
say nothing
and be nothing.*

—Aristotle

Chapter 34

THE MAGGOT MIRACLE

Courage to See the Good through the Bad

When I entered Madge's room, I smelled something malodorous.

"Doctor, my foot wiggles," she said. Madge had returned to the office after a missed appointment.

"It must be your diabetic neuropathy," I responded. "When your nerves are damaged, you can have a tickling sensation in your feet."

She nodded.

"Have you changed your dressing?" I asked.

"No, I haven't. Not since I was here two weeks ago."

I looked at her bandage, soiled and dirty, covering the wound on her foot.

She looked into my eyes and smirked, anticipating another lecture.

Not wanting to disappoint my patient's expectations, I let her have it. "Don't you remember what I told you? Because of your diabetes, you must look at your feet every day. And you need to change your dressing daily—without exception."

She reluctantly nodded.

I unwrapped the gauze to examine the foot I had debrided two weeks earlier. The reeking smell of pus and decaying flesh reached my nostrils and then lingered in my sinuses. I felt lightheaded and nauseated as I unrolled the layers of gauze. I hesitated for a moment and then sneezed to rid myself of the putrid fog—only to have it drift back into my consciousness.

A sea of white covered the wound. At first, I thought it was necrotic tissue. But on closer inspection, I noticed a blanket of white material wiggled on her foot. Small white worms were nibbling away at her flesh. Festering maggots.

My stomach churned like a washing machine.

Puzzled by my silence, she asked, "Is everything okay?"

I watched the little white worms squirming around on her wound, wondering how someone could be so lackadaisical about their health. I thought about how to respond. I remembered what they told me in medical school. "Good doctors wear a poker face." No circumstance should shake a physician's calm, controlled demeanor.

But it was too late. Without a doubt, my patient had already seen my anxious, perturbed, and unsettled face.

I held my breath, cleaned off the maggots and examined her toe. With each layer of worms I removed, I noticed something remarkable. Her wound appeared spotless, without a hint of dead or necrotic tissue. It looked better than it did the last time she visited the office. The maggots had performed a miracle.

"The wound looks good, but I think we need a home health nurse to come and change your dressing. *Every day*," I added.

Madge returned the following week. The wound on her foot had healed completely. Dumbfounded, I researched the topic of maggots and wounds. Ninety years ago, maggots were the treatment of choice for non-healing wounds. Dr. Baer, an orthopedic surgeon at Johns Hopkins, pioneered maggot debridement therapy on children with chronic bone infections. Practicing during World War I, the old army doctor noticed how wounded soldiers left in the trenches fared better than the ones taken straight to the hospital for treatment. The soldiers receiving immediate treatment at the hospital died of infection, but the ones left for dead in the field were often healed of their wounds. The difference? Maggots.

In World War I, the flies, not the medics, were the first responders in the trenches. They flew to the rescue, laying larvae in the open wounds of soldiers. Their larvae hatched into maggots, eating away the dying flesh and preventing a nidus for infection. As a result, many lives were saved.

Think of it this way: hundreds of super-specialized microsurgeons are working around the clock, debriding away the dead flesh, leaving healthy tissue behind.

Positively elegant.

Using this analogy, what are the maggots in our lives? What are the things that seem to feed on our souls?

Our initial response to those maggots is negative. We feel like upchucking. The trauma of a wound is enough, but wriggling worms on dying flesh brings our suffering to another level.

What about you? Do you ever feel like God piles afflictions on top of each other? Discouraged, do you ever wonder how much more you can endure.

A Joyful Outlook

Be of good courage. God's methods of healing our wounds often make us uncomfortable, on the surface, appearing as grotesque worms. Yet underneath, the old and the dead are eaten away, allowing us to be made new.

Learn to look below the surface and marvel at the transformation. The most unpleasant, hideous experiences may be the very things that bring you healing, wholeness, and renewal.

Give God Permission to Work

Remember the maggot miracle. The Great Physician is always working for our good. However, we must let Him complete His work. The word *let* may be the most difficult word in the English language. Spiritually speaking, letting means giving God consent to work in whatever way He chooses. Like signing a consent form to let the surgeon do *whatever it takes* to fix the problem, we relinquish control. If we want restoration, we must submit, surrender and watch the worms wiggle away.

"Consider it pure joy, my brothers and sisters, whenever you face trials of many kinds, because you know that the testing of your faith produces perseverance. Let perseverance finish its work so that you may be mature and complete, not lacking anything." [57]

Hardship prepares ordinary people
for an extraordinary destiny.

—C S Lewis

Adversity is not a simple tool. It is God's most effective tool for the advancement of our spiritual lives. The circumstances and events that we see as setbacks are oftentimes the very things that launch us into periods of intense spiritual growth. Once we begin to understand this and accept it as a spiritual fact of life, adversity becomes easier to bear.

—Charles Stanley

Chapter 35

SHADOWS IN THE VALLEY

Courage to Persevere

I was in Stone Mountain, Georgia, on vacation, laying on my back under my travel trailer, trying to open the grey water line. The gravel seemed to cut through my clothes. Covered in sweat and smelling like sewage, I wondered why I had bought the trailer in the first place. Something always needed to be fixed. Exasperated, I looked at my wife and kids, patiently playing frisbee, waiting for me to unclog the toilet so we could get ready for the evening's fireworks display.

A stranger walked up to my trailer to give me some pointers. "Try pushing it in again. All the way this time. Then pull it hard. Sometimes the flow gets blocked."

I followed his instructions. A gushing sound resulted. The blocked sewage began moving down the tubes into the septic tank. The kids cheered, dropped the frisbee and raced to the bathroom. I never knew flushing the toilet could generate such excitement.

My wife gave me one of those, *I told you so,* expressions. She thanked the stranger and headed back inside the trailer. Before leaving, she said, "See, all you had to do was ask for help."

The man must have read my *how did you know that* look, as I rolled out from under the trailer.

He chuckled. "That's the crazy thing about RVs and travel trailers. You drive a while. Then you work a while. Then you repeat the cycle all over again."

I stood up, offered him a handshake, and thanked him for the advice. He received my dirty, soot-covered hand and shook it firmly, showing no concern about where my hands had been. "I'm Bob," he said.

Our small talk grew into an in-depth conversation. Bob shared part of his story. "I remember sitting at home, trying to eat. I didn't have the strength to lift a spoon to my mouth. I told my wife, 'I can't do this anymore.' Norma looked me straight in the eye and said, 'Yes, Bob, you can. We're going to grow old together.'"

Bob continued. "I was so weak, I couldn't do anything for myself. I had lost the will to live. I kept asking myself, *How can this be happening to me? I'm a pastor. I've devoted my whole life to visiting the sick in the hospital. Don't I deserve a get-out-of-jail-free card?*"

He paused for a moment. "I asked God, 'This is the thanks I get?' I had never been on the other end of suffering. All the times I had encouraged, prayed, and comforted others. And now it was my turn."

He shuffled his feet before continuing. "My wife kept bringing me back to reality. She would tell me, 'We'll throw a pity party for you later, dear. Now swallow another spoonful of eggs.'"

"What made you so sick?" I said.

"My life spiraled downward from the moment I received the diagnosis: acute leukemia. First came the weight loss. Then came the complications of chemotherapy. Malnutrition. Infections. Pneumonia. Diarrhea. Loss of energy. I learned the hard way, it's not the cancer that kills, but the treatment. Seventy-five days in the intensive care unit sapped every ounce of strength from my body. The bone marrow transplant left me with no immune system. I was emotionally, physically, and spiritually exhausted. I gave up. But God, my wife, and my doctors didn't give up on me."

Then Bob smiled. "You're looking at a walking miracle."

Down in the Valley

Did you know a place called the Shadow of Death really exists? Historians suggest the valley rests on the east side of Jerusalem, a narrow, deep ravine on the road between Jericho and the Holy City. David survived the valley and lived to tell about it, but someone greater than David walked through this wasteland: His name is Jesus.

Going to the cross, our Savior walked through the valley before entering the eastern gate of Jerusalem to complete His work. After that journey, He died in in our place, thereby giving us the opportunity to receive life, forgiveness, and power. Because He suffered on the cross, evil is no longer something we should fear.

Ten years later, Bob still tells everyone his story. He relates how his near-death experiences strengthened his faith. He told me how others nursed him back to health. Bob reminded me of several truths to remember when walking through death's valley.

We Are Not Promised a Life Free of Suffering

Pain is part of living in a fallen world; even Jesus suffered. Nevertheless, through the power of the cross, Christ transformed our afflictions by His sacrifice. We can demonstrate God's power in us, proving His goodness, adequacy, and faithfulness, whatever circumstances we encounter.

For One Who Believes in Christ, Death Is Only a Shadow

Sometimes, death's shadow overwhelms us. The shadow is real, yet it has no real power. The silhouette of death discourages, intimidates, and isolates. It makes us feel forgotten, but it cannot separate God's children from His love.

The Scriptures remind us that we walk *through* the dark valley. Suffering lasts only for a season. But because of the cross, the shadow of death is only a place on the way to our final destination. By faith, we must walk through the valley, following in the footsteps of our Savior.

We Walk by Faith, Not Explanations

Our finite minds can't completely grasp the meaning of our suffering. The great *why* question can't always be answered here on earth. Sufficient for the day is the adequacy of His promises. They are the solid ground we walk upon.

God Promises His Presence

Nothing, not even physical death, can separate believers from the love of Christ. Come what may, God walks with us through death's shadow, protecting us from harm, giving us grace to endure our affliction, and helping us in our time of need.

So, let's be strong and of good courage. Let's keep walking through the valley. Our Savior has already been there and paved the way. Death's shadow no longer has power over us if we believe in Christ.

"Even though I walk through the valley of the shadow of death, I will fear no evil, for you are with me." [58]

*The best way out
is always through.*

—Robert Frost

I walked a mile with Pleasure,
She chattered all the way,
But left me none the wiser,
For all she had to say.

I walked a mile with Sorrow,
And ne'er a word said she,
But oh, the things I learned from her,
When Sorrow walked with me.

—J. R. Miller

Chapter 36

THE BULLETPROOF VEST

Courage to Live

I went to the preoperative area as the nurses prepared the operating room. A young lady, about to have her gallbladder removed, lay in the bed. Her husband sat beside her. She clutched the guardrail of the bed like someone holding on to the lap bar of a rollercoaster just as it crests the top of the hill.

Trying to ease the tension, I started a little small talk. I reached out my hand to shake her husband's. With one hand he held his wife's purse. In the other, he clutched a baby, looking like a fullback carrying a football.

He nodded and apologized. "Hi, I'm Sam. Sorry. My hands are full."

The baby whimpered. I watched the father whisper into the baby's ear.

"Shh." He rocked the child back and forth in his arm, reassuring his wife that he was up to the challenge.

I pointed at the baby. "Boy or girl?"

"He's all boy, sir."

His response puzzled me. "No one says *sir* anymore. Did you serve in the military?"

He nodded. "Yes, sir. Infantry division."

"Were you ever deployed?"

"Yes, sir. Two years in Iraq."

We prayed for a successful surgery. After the prayer, I noticed a change in Sam's countenance.

He had an intense look in his eyes, like someone who had experienced some tough times.

Sam put the baby on his shoulder and gently patted his son's back. "I am not afraid," he said.

I turned and headed toward the operating room, wondering what he had experienced in Iraq.

Thirty minutes later, I returned to the soldier to give him the good news—another boring gallbladder surgery. I repeated my routine postoperative talk, giving instructions and answering questions. I stood up and turned for the door.

Before I could leave, the soldier interrupted. "Doctor, you got a minute?"

I looked down at the baby, now sleeping on the sofa. "Sam, tell me a little more about Iraq?"

Sam stared at the wall and told his story with little emotion, as if he were describing an out-of-body experience. "It was a typical day in Iraq. At 120 degrees, the heat makes you feel like a piece of fried bacon. My team was on patrol, walking down a crowded street in Fallujah. It happened so fast; I didn't realize what happened. I heard a horrifying sound and felt an excruciating pain in my chest. Then everything turned black. I came back to consciousness long enough to realize my team was dragging me through the street to shelter. The sound of bullets whizzed by my head. My buddies threw me into an armored truck. The pain in my chest overwhelmed me, and I passed out again."

He looked straight into my eyes. "It wasn't until later I put everything together. A rooftop sniper shot me right in the chest from four hundred yards. My unit risked their lives to save mine. Thank God I was wearing my bulletproof vest."

His face fell. "Now I suffer from post-traumatic stress disorder (PTSD). I can be in the most peaceful surroundings, and without warning, I feel an overwhelming sense of paranoia. I have the feeling someone is going to shoot me. I can never let my defenses down—even when I'm sleeping."

Trying to wrap my mind around Sam's experience, I asked another question. "How are you coping with your disability?"

"Great. My psychiatrist cannot explain my progress. I am a Christian and know that God works all things out for good. I now counsel other soldiers who suffer with the same problems. Several have asked me, "*How can I live like this?*" I remind them, that is the point. *They are alive.* When you're breathing, there's always hope."

Our Bulletproof Vest

What I learned from that young man is, life hurts. People and circumstances afflict us with painful memories. Our enemies aim for the heart. Satan's darts hit the bull's-eye, wounding deeply, leaving us injured. We suffer loneliness, abandonment, and regret. We fear the future. We suffer loss of relationships. Hurtful words are forever imprinted on our memory. No one dodges these emotional bullets.

Despite this, there's good news for those who believe in a greater truth. Christ has given us a bulletproof vest. This vest of protection cannot take away the pain, but it can transform our afflictions.

"For I am convinced that neither death, nor life, nor angels, nor principalities, nor things present, nor things to come, nor powers, nor height, nor depth, nor any other created thing, will be able to separate us from the love of God, which is in Christ Jesus our Lord. [59]

Believers sometimes need Sam's reminder—we are alive in Christ. A sneaky sniper can't snuff the life out of the Christian. Our union with Jesus is so strong, nothing can separate us from His love and His life. Whatever comes, God's love gives life, under any circumstance. For the Christian, even death cannot separate us. Although painful experiences can hurt us, because of Jesus, they cannot harm us.

Are you wearing your bulletproof vest? Are you fully aware that you have received eternal life? You can do *nothing* to deserve it, but *nothing* can take it away.

The Game-Changer

Our bulletproof vest changes the game. Christ finished the battle, won the victory, and defeated our enemies. He is our covering.

Through Him, we are triumphant, hard-pressed, but not crushed. Perplexed, but not in despair.[60] Because of Christ's power in us, that which initially wounds us, will strengthen us in the end.

"I have come so that they may have life, and have it to the full." [61]

__Courage__
__isn't having the strength to go on.__
__It's going on__
__when you don't have the strength.__

—Napolean Bonaparte

It's always too early to quit.

—Norman Vincent Peale

Chapter 37

THE RIGHT STUFF

Courage to Live for Others

A lice came to the office requesting weight loss surgery. When I entered the room, I didn't see what I expected. A man in his sixties was hunched over in the chair, wheezing, coughing, and gasping for breath. He looked like a shriveled raisin. His wife Alice sat on the examination table. In comparison to her husband, she appeared healthy. Overweight, but hearty and full of energy.

"Can you staple my stomach?" she asked. "I need to lose one hundred pounds."

In her arms, Alice held a two-year-old boy, covered in dirt, trying to wiggle free from her grasp. The toddler squealed. Embarrassed, she released him. The boy waddled over to his grandpa, climbed into his lap, and reached for his cell phone.

I looked again at the chart, making sure I had the right patient. Wanting to lighten things up, I pointed to the toddler. "I know who's boss in this family."

The man laughed, hacked up some phlegm, and turned blue.

"Do you need some oxygen?" I asked.

He took a deep breath and exhaled, pursing his lips. "Forget I'm here."

For a moment, I considered calling an ambulance, but I drew my focus back on the issue at hand. Maybe I could finish the evaluation *before* he stopped breathing. I asked the most important question first. "Alice, why do you want to lose weight?"

"My husband's sick," she replied.

"Yes." I nodded. "I recognize that, but you're the one requesting surgery. Do I need to remind you of all the potential complications of having half your stomach removed? There are many reasons to desire weight loss surgery. Why do you want to take this risk?"

"Doctor, I know about the complications." Alice pointed to her grandson. "I'm doing this for him." The toddler played with a cell phone resting on his granddad's lap, unaware the discussion centered on his future.

Confused, I asked her for an explanation.

Her husband interjected, "I have lung cancer. The oncologist says I have three months to live. We're raising our grandson, Zach. His mom left him with us one day and never came back."

I tried to grasp the gravity of their circumstances. Struggling to breathe with terminal cancer is enough of a struggle, but the possibility of leaving your grandkids uncared for heavies one's mind.

For a moment, silence filled the room. Then Grandma added, "I don't want to live without my husband, but I have to, for Zach. My weight slows me down. I can't keep up with our grandson. I need to be around for at least sixteen more years, till Zach graduates."

Grandma had to press on, knowing she would raise her grandson without the help of her husband of forty years. Whatever it took. Undergoing a high-risk surgery and enduring the loneliness without her soul mate, Alice committed herself to provide for her grandson's future, alone in her golden years.

Alice had good reason to carry on, but what motivates the rest of us to live? Sometimes, we desire health only to be delivered from suffering. We don't want to go through the pain of dying. But we must change our perspective. The life we're given comes with a plan.

Living for Christ and Living for Others

The greatest reason for living involves fulfilling God's purposes for our lives. If we concentrate on honoring Him in our adversity, then everything else falls into place. In a prison cell, Paul reminded others he was ready to experience heaven. *"To live is Christ and to die is gain."*[62] For the Christian facing death, either way—death or life—God promises victory. God honors the life that honors Him.

The apostle Paul, physically wasting away in prison, wanted to end his torment and graduate to heaven. And yet, he carried on for the benefit of his friends. He endured hardship so that others could grow in their faith. What inspires us to press on through our adversity? The greatest reason to carry on is to live for Christ by living for others.

Honoring God by serving people should be the Christian's obsession. It is our greatest, highest, and most noble purpose, in health or in sickness. Like the grandmother who needed her health to care for her grandchild alone, no matter the difficulty, we should pour the life Christ has given us, into serving others.

"But I am hard pressed from both directions, having the desire to depart and be with Christ; for that is very much better; yet to remain on the flesh is more necessary for your sake." [63]

I eagerly expect and hope that I will in no way be ashamed, but will have sufficient courage so that now as always Christ will be exalted in my body, whether by life or by death.
For to me, to live is Christ and to die is gain.
If I am to go on living in this body, this will mean fruitful labor for me.
Yet what shall I choose? I do not know!
I am torn between the two: I desire to depart and be with Christ, which is better by far; but it is more necessary for you that I remain in the body." [64]

—The Apostle Paul

Chapter 38

HIS STORY, HER STORY

Courage to Receive Your Healing

God always heals, but not always according to our expectations. I walked into the intensive care unit to visit my friend, Todd. He stood next to Destiny's bedside, caressing her hair, trying to look brave. The breathing machine forced oxygen into his wife's lungs. The monitors beeped incessantly, drowning out the noise of the television. The nurse turned off the alarms and walked out into the hallway.

I shook Todd's hand. "I heard things aren't going well for Destiny."

Todd rubbed his eyes and scratched his unshaved face. He grabbed his wife's hand, wrinkled his forehead and looked intently into my eyes. "Is it okay to ask God to heal Destiny? You know better than anyone everything she has been through." Todd paused and ran his hand through his hair. "Or am I being selfish?"

I didn't know what to say, so I kept quiet.

After several seconds of silence, Todd told his story. "Eight years ago, I developed severe headaches. Then my vision blurred. I began having seizures. They found a tumor on the right side of my brain. Destiny and I prayed, asking God for healing."

Todd looked at his wife and then hesitated. Tears filled his eyes. "Before surgery, the neurosurgeon ordered another MRI. The day before surgery, he called me on the phone. My brain tumor vanished." Todd smiled. "The brain surgeon said he had never seen a case like mine before. Praise God, I've been cancer-free for eight years."

The respiratory therapist came in the room and suctioned out the fluid in Destiny's lungs. Destiny coughed and Todd walked over to comfort his wife. He ran his fingers through her long black hair doing his best to comfort her. "She's only thirty-two years old and has suffered so much."

I looked at Destiny taking guppy breaths through the breathing tube. After her gastric bypass in Mexico, her health spiraled out of control. She developed chronic nausea and vomiting, which could not be controlled with medications. Her weight loss far exceeded the norm for her type of surgery.

Then came two more operations by two different surgeons. The operations were successful, but she didn't improve. Instead, her medical condition worsened.

In desperation, she came to me for a fourth surgical opinion. Realizing another surgery would only make her worse, we tried to get the right team together to manage her problems. She developed several rare conditions with long names, treated with nontraditional therapies. After a long and difficult search, modern medicine had no solutions to offer Destiny.

What started as a doctor-patient relationship soon transformed into a friendship. Several months had passed since I had seen her professionally. In that period, her body had wasted away to eighty pounds.

Todd interrupted my thoughts. "I feel as though a part of me is dying. Destiny believed I would be healed, against all odds. We have two young children. How will we make it without her?"

Then Todd asked another tough question. "Do you think Destiny will be healed? That's what I'm praying for."

I hesitated again, afraid to say what looked obvious. Destiny had a grim prognosis. I remembered an expression used by one of my mentors, Dr. Debakey. When pushed into a corner with a puzzling question, he would say, "Only God knows that answer."

Without thinking, I repeated the phrase to Todd.

He remained silent, pondered my statement, and massaged his wife's foot.

Looking at the monitors, I thought about the cliché I had uttered. I remembered how Debakey used the phrase to sidestep tough subjects. The *only God knows* axiom was a cop-out. A getaway phrase.

Alarms went off, pulling my mind back to the present. I silenced the monitors and looked at Destiny. "Todd, you know that if God were to heal her of her present problems, you would still have lots of other issues to overcome."

Todd grabbed Destiny's hand, then mine, and prayed. "God, you do know what is best for Destiny. And since you know, help me to know what to ask for. You healed me from my brain cancer and I know you can heal Destiny. Show me your will. Teach me how to pray for her."

Todd's insightful prayer left me stunned. Todd had taken the appropriate step, asking God to reveal His purposes in their situation.

Over the next several days, Destiny continued to deteriorate. Her feet became mottled from poor circulation. Her kidneys failed. But Todd continued to pray. In time, Todd realized how God was answering his prayers—according to His will, not Todd's.

God did heal Destiny. She passed on ahead of Todd. Freed from her misery, Destiny entered the splendor of God's presence, where no more sickness, suffering, pain, medications or breathing machines exist. God healed her—completely.

Faith is Flexible

Jumping to false conclusions about God's will can leave us confused. When prayers aren't answered according to *our* expectations, we question our faith, God's goodness and the certainty of His promises. Don't assume you know God's will when asking Him to intervene. Don't misplace your faith.

Since God has a plan, ask Him to reveal it to you. If we lack wisdom, we can ask. God promises to show us how to respond in tough circumstances. He will give us insight, perception and understanding, showing us how to direct our requests.

Introspection and Illumination

We must examine our motives. Sometimes, our requests are self-centered instead of God-centered. We pray for a cure because it alleviates *our* suffering, gives *us* comfort and relieves *our* pain. Like a child, coming to their father with an immature request, we ask with a selfish agenda. Our wise, all-knowing, Heavenly Father says, "I love you enough to say no."

One thing is certain: God knows. He knows the plans He has for our lives. He knows what we need before we ask. He knows the hairs on our head. He knows the thoughts in our minds before they ever become words. And our Father in Heaven has no intention of leaving us in the dark about His will.

We can emulate Todd's prayer. Let's ask for His guidance on how to pray. God has promised to answer the believer's prayer centered in His will. So, why not ask for a God's-eye view of our situation? He wants to show us, with specificity, what to ask for.

Faith Is Firm

In life's uncertain situations, we can cling to certainties in His word, where He gives more than five thousand promises. They are dependable, accurate and trustworthy. Which ones are you claiming for your situation?

God Promises to Heal

Often, we are shortsighted in understanding the depth of God's promises. He does heal *all* our diseases, but in His timing, in His way, and for His purposes.

> *"Praise the Lord, oh my soul, and forget not all His benefits—who forgives all your sins and heals all your diseases…"* [65]

The story of Todd and Destiny brings out different facets of the unsearchable wisdom of God. In Todd's case, God chose the miraculous: a healing that defied explanation. But for Destiny, God healed her in eternity, releasing her from suffering.

Faith Like a Diamond

There are no formulas to prayer. Like light shining through a multifaceted diamond, faith can be expressed in many ways. Faith can be demonstrated by asking for healing on this side of heaven—or the other. God is God. He knows the plans for us and we can be confident in His promises, rest assured in His will.

> *"Now faith is the confidence in what we hope for and assurance about what we do not see."*[66]

"Life can only be understood backwards; but it must be lived forwards."

—Soren Kierkegaard

Chapter 39

LIVING WITH THE UNKNOWN

Courage in Uncertainty

B rent stirred cream into his coffee. "The neurologist told me I would be in a wheelchair within a year. And the way I was feeling, I believed him."

I sipped a cup of Joe and listened to Brent's story.

"Six months prior to my diagnosis, I felt a little sting in my leg. I thought it was my back." Brent grabbed his wife's hand. "Then the muscles in my arms began to twitch and my balance was affected. I think we saw a million doctors and spent a million dollars." He laughed. "I guess I'm like that lady in the Bible. She suffered much in the hands of many doctors. But when I fell and broke my wrist, I knew something was really wrong."

Brent paused and put his arm around Sheila. "Finally, we found a neurologist who figured it out: chronic inflammatory demyelinating polyradiculoneuropathy. CIDP for short."

I chuckled. "I'm a surgeon, could you translate that for me."

Brent continued, "I guess the longer the name, the less doctors know about it. It's like losing the insulation on an electrical wire. Without the insulation on your nerves, the messages get crossed.

"The doctor told me, 'I know what you have, but there's little more I can tell you. No one can predict how you'll respond to treatment and if you'll ever go into remission. We don't really know how you got the disease, but it may have been a reaction to a flu shot.'" Brent stared into his coffee. "The only thing I knew for certain was uncertainty."

I listened as Brent described how each treatment failed. His doctors tried exchange transfusions and plasmapheresis. Meanwhile, his small business began to crumble. Brent had to dip into his son's college fund to pay medical bills. The responsibilities of life were pressing down on him, hard. There seemed to be no end to his obstacles. But I noticed, while Brent recalled tragic circumstances, he kept bringing up several things he learned.

God Is in Control

Humanly speaking, control is only an illusion—smoke and mirrors. Brent anchored his life in this truth when facing uncertainty: God is in control and we aren't. Job asked God *why* he suffered sixteen times, but he never received an answer to his question. Instead, God reminded Job of His sovereignty.[67] Like Job, Brent confessed, "Come what may, God controls your life, your situation, and your destiny."

The Purpose for Suffering

Our feelings will deceive us. Our pain whispers, "*God doesn't care. Suffering has no purpose.*" In those times of doubt, Brent reminded himself that only God sees the big picture. For Job to pass the test, he couldn't have known the reason for his suffering. Job had to demonstrate faith without knowing about the cosmic debate in heaven.

Like Job, and like Brent, we may never know the reason for our troubles while we're on Earth. God wants us to trust Him and respond in faith. When we stand firm, we show others how our loving God strengthens us, provides for our needs, and gives us peace.

Believe in God's Faithfulness

Through his season of uncertainty, Brent learned to hold onto God's faithful promises. His first set of treatments were unsuccessful. Next, came the expensive intravenous gamma globulin therapy, but still no cure. After Brent ran out of insurance, the doctors tried a round of steroids. Within a week, the feeling mysteriously returned in Brent's legs. The doctors were puzzled as to how the steroids worked. They couldn't explain how Brent went into remission. Within three months, Brent was his old self.

"He who calls you is faithful; he will surely do it." [68]

A Deeper Experience of God

Like Job, Brent reached the other side of his personal mountain with more questions than answers.

When Brent finished his last sip of coffee, he said, "I guess I stand in awe of who God is these days. I praise Him more now than ever. I am more contented than I was before I got sick. I know what it truly means to be thankful."

Brent never understood the meaning of his suffering, but like Job, he grew in his understanding of God. At the end, Job confessed.

"My ears had heard of you, but now my eyes have seen you." [69]

A Richer Experience of Life

Brent recovered, but not without scars. No one knows how he got CIPD and no one can explain why it went into remission. After suffering for so long, Brent really doesn't care how he was delivered. He received a second chance, an opportunity to live life again.

"I take advantage of each moment. My relationships are richer and deeper than before. And I've learned to enjoy the little things."

If God were to bless us with another opportunity to be healthy, how would we respond? Would our attitudes improve with our second chance, or would we choose to focus on why we were struck?

We must relinquish control to God. Let's face it, He's running things anyway. Learn to experience God in new ways. Accept everything from His hand. Receive the fullness of grace. That's where the good life begins.

"So do not fear, for I am with you; do not be dismayed, for I am your God. I will strengthen you and help you; I will uphold you with my righteous right hand." [70]

***When nothing is sure,
everything is possible.***

—Margaret Drabble

Chapter 40
PROMISES FOR UNCERTAIN TIMES

"We have this hope as an anchor for the soul, firm and secure." [71]

"Heal me, LORD, and I will be healed; save me and I will be saved, for you are the one I praise." [72]

"Cast your cares on the LORD and he will sustain you; he will never let the righteous be shaken." [73]

"The righteous cry out, and the LORD hears them; he delivers them from all their troubles." [74]

"No, in all these things we are more than conquerors through him that loved us." [75]

"You gave me life and showed me kindness, and in your providence watched over my spirit." [76]

Chapter 41

PECANS IN HEAVEN

Courage to Give Life to Others

E veryone will die one day, but not everyone will truly live.
I first met Katherine in the emergency room, but her problem
wasn't urgent. She had cancer on her breast, which had been
festering for months. Her daughters, startled by the grotesque-looking
mass on her chest, whisked her away to be seen immediately. Katherine
was in no hurry. She already knew her diagnosis.

When I voiced my concerns about her cancer, she seemed indifferent.
She comforted her adult children. "Everything is okay. I will be all right."
Then, out of nowhere, she asked a silly question. "Can I pick pecans in
the morning?"

Her daughters, frustrated by their mother's detached emotions,
asked a question. "How long has this cancer been present?"

I looked at Katherine's innocent expression, then spoke to her kids. "Several years."

Starting Cancer Treatments

To everyone's surprise, Katherine consented to the usual treatments: surgery, chemotherapy and radiation. But she endured them for a different reason than most.

She underwent treatment not for herself, but for her children. Over time, I began to understand her. She was not indifferent, indecisive, or noncompliant. She simply didn't think of herself at all. Her depth of spiritual maturity had progressed to a level where life centered around others, not herself.

With each office visit, she brought gifts in paper sacks. "Thank you, Doctor. Here's a sack of pecans. I picked them in the Angelina River bottom."

Katherine never asked questions about her cancer. Our discussions focused on her pecan picking. For Katherine, a life worth living came from her time spent at the river. The muddy Angelina River bottom was her chapel. There she prayed, meditated, and thought of ways to encourage others. Katherine's greatest joy came from her daily walks by the riverbank, gathering pecans, where she basked in her time with the Lord.

While I treated Katherine, my mother developed lung cancer. I watched her shrivel like a wilting flower with each dose of chemotherapy. My mother's situation left me discouraged, frustrated, and feeling utterly helpless. I performed life-saving operations for others, yet could do nothing for this woman I treasured.

However, God scheduled a divine appointment for a discouraged doctor—a heavenly cure for my self-pity. It came in little sacks of pecans. Once, Katherine came into the exam room, placed the pecans in my hands, and started her interrogation.

"Your nurse told me about your mother's cancer. How is she? I've been praying for her down by the river."

I opened the sack of pecans and cracked one open with my boot. "Thank you, I love pecans."

I looked at Katherine's face, full of contentment, peace, and life. I had never made the connection before, but in her face, I saw my mother.

In a strange sort of way, I felt I was helping my mother by helping Katherine. Through Katherine, I gained comfort, encouragement, and hope. It strengthened me to think that someone, perhaps my mother's oncologist, was extending grace to her, like I tried to do for Katherine.

Maybe they were giving what I could not give.

I imagined my mother, like Katherine, returning the favor, offering life, comfort, and strength to some discouraged health care worker—an unending cycle of giving and receiving.

Over the next year, Katherine's medical appointments became times of fellowship for the both of us. Her conversation gravitated to my mother and her condition. In these moments, I wondered. Why would someone dying from metastatic cancer be concerned about someone else's chemotherapy? Who was helping whom?

Instead of giving, I felt I was always on the receiving side when Katherine came for her doctor's visit.

The day came when Katherine was hospitalized for pneumonia. I stopped by on rounds to visit. "Lady, where are my pecans?"

She coughed and did her best to smile. "I'll bring you some when I get out of here."

Katherine knew her time was coming. "It's getting close, isn't it, Doctor? By the way, how is your mother doing?"

I sighed. "She's in hospice now. The chemo isn't working anymore."

"She's going to be fine. I'll pray for her." Katherine coughed again. "I'm ready to go. Don't let them put me on a breathing machine. Let me go when it's my time."

But *I* wasn't ready to see her go. So, I changed the subject. "Hey, did you know that my mother loves pecans?"

"Imagine that," she said sarcastically. "I'll pick her a bag too."

It wasn't long until both Katherine and my mother passed into eternity. The following year, I walked into my office to find a garbage bag filled with pecans sitting on my desk. Fastened on top of the bag was a card, the address read: *from Heaven*. I rocked back in my chair, cracked a pecan, and studied the postcard. *"We promised Mother that we would bring you some. One of her last wishes was to bring you fresh pecans every year."* I peeled off the hull and thought about Katherine and the comfort she gave.

What Is Comfort?

When we think of comfort, we might picture someone trying to calm a crying baby. We rock them to sleep, give them a bottle and sing them a lull-a-bye. But comfort, as defined in the scriptures, suggests more than a burp and a diaper change to smooth things over. This word embodies more than a tranquil feeling when life's problems disappear. Real comfort comes when one is encouraged, strengthened and empowered to thrive in the midst of their struggles. God's comfort doesn't kill the pain. It helps us endure patiently, respond magnanimously and live victoriously through our difficulty.

Jesus left us with the Comforter, the Holy Spirit. He lives inside us and will guide us through our trials.

One Reason for Suffering

Like Katherine, one purpose of your challenges may be to strengthen others.

When you receive God's encouragement, you can spread it around. When you receive grace, you should extend it.

Your darkest hours may be there to brighten someone else's path by your example. Suffering gives us an opportunity to help others who are hurting. How refreshing to see someone who realizes their circumstances are there so they can help others.

The apostle Paul said it this way:

"If we are distressed, it is for your comfort and salvation, if we are comforted it is for your comfort…" [77]

How it Flows

Katherine knew a secret. She received heavenly strength when she channeled it to others. She encouraged others by giving them pecans. If you will exhort others, then God will empower you in return. He strengthens our inner man, the part that doesn't decay.[78] God doesn't comfort us so we can sit on our blessed assurance. Comfort flows from the Spirit—to us and then through us—into others. Perhaps God would boost our spirits more often if we exhorted those who are in desperate need of it.

Focusing on Others

Katherine comforted me by focusing on my troubles rather than on her own. She could have obsessed about her cancer, her pain and her problems. Instead, she asked questions about my mother, someone she didn't know. She prayed for my needs, instead of her own.

We should think more of others and less of ourselves. Begin by listening, hearing and learning about their life challenges.

God's comfort is all inclusive. We don't need to be an expert in someone's circumstances to offer encouragement. All kinds of people are experiencing all kinds of trials, and each of them needs someone to care.

"...and the God of all comfort, who comforts us in all our troubles so that we can comfort those in any trouble with the comfort we ourselves receive from God." [79]

Infused with God's strength, Paul helped people in *any* trouble. The God of all Comfort, through Paul's afflictions, empowered him to build up, no matter their situation. The apostle spread encouragement without discrimination.

There are only two prerequisites for imparting encouragement—having experienced suffering and having received heavenly comfort.

You may not know what it's like to lose a child, suffer from brain cancer or have your breast removed. But if you have attended any session in the school of suffering, then you are equipped to impart comfort. Your unique story of how grace has pulled you through your tough times can help another soul.

Tell others about it. Explain what you have learned through your adversity. Offer insights into your feelings and emotions during your darkest times. Share quotes, stories, or scriptures that strengthened your faith. Pray with them. Send them texts. Let them know you are thinking about them. But don't stay silent.

What qualifies you to exhort others? God's grace working through your experiences.

Everyone has something to give. Katherine gave bags of pecans.

Spread encouragement. Express empathy. Learn to weep with those who weep and mourn with those who mourn. If you share your sufferings with others, God will abundantly comfort you.

"And our hope for you is firm, because we know that just as you share in our sufferings, so also you share in our comfort." [80]

The miracle is this:
the more we share, the more we have.

—Leonard Nimoy

Continue knocking
on Heaven's door.
Its hinges have not rusted.

Chapter 42

A BAGFUL OF PENNIES AND A CAT SCAN

Courage to Be Persistent

I remember the day a five-foot-two Hispanic lady, who couldn't speak English, taught this stubborn surgeon a lesson in persistence. I entered the room surprised to see a young Hispanic boy sitting on the exam table. I did a double take and looked back at my records. The chart indicated my patient was a thirty-eight-year-old female named Enid. The nine-year-old smiled and pointed to his mother. "She's the patient."

Enid hid herself in the corner, so much that I failed to notice her when I walked into the room. Her hand-sewn dress appeared faded but clean. Her shoes were well-worn. A plastic bag full of change sat by her purse.

I introduced myself and reached out my hand. With timidity, she followed suit and shook it. She didn't say a word, but her strong grip spoke volumes. Her calloused hands, hardened by years of labor, told me more than the twenty-eight pages of medical records I had just reviewed.

She gazed at the floor, trying not to make eye contact. "No hablo Ingles." Embarrassed, she looked toward her son, prodding him to tell her story.

I rubbed the boy's head. "What is your name?"

"My name is Ricardo, but you can call me Ricky."

Ricky had been brought along to interpret for his mother—a frequent practice for first-generation immigrants.

"How can I help you?"

Ricky pointed again at his mother. "She still hurts. They took out her gallbladder two months ago and her pain is getting worse."

Since obtaining a history through an interpreter was time-consuming, I backtracked through the medical chart, reviewed all the tests and read the operative reports. By all appearances, her previous doctors had done everything right. The operation had been successful, but the patient had not improved.

I felt like a backup quarterback called in to replace the injured first stringer, now trailing by two touchdowns. I studied the chart again, performed a thorough examination and tried to piece together Enid's complicated history.

I was unsure what Enid expected. I had no Hail Mary pass in the two-minute warning. Her previous doctors had given her good care, but Enid was still losing ground.

"It looks like your doctors did a thorough job. Everything has been managed appropriately," I said to Ricky. "I wouldn't have done anything different. Why didn't you go back to the surgeon who performed her operation?" Ricky interpreted my words back to his mom and then interjected. "She did go back several times, but they didn't listen. They told her everything was okay."

I knew better than to throw stones at the other surgeon. What goes around, comes around.

I said. "I have enough trouble trying to explain some of my own outcomes, let alone someone else's. I don't know how or if I can help you."

I looked at Enid's face as she listened to Ricky interpret my words. Her shy expression changed to one of anger, frustration, and determination. I could tell by her frown, she understood more English than she let on. Like a machine gun, she fired out a blast of words in Spanish, telling her son to translate. I stopped Ricky before he could respond. I replied to her in Spanish. "Claro que si! I understand what you are saying."

Enid and Ricky were silent, shocked that I spoke Spanish. A look of fear now covered Enid's face. She was afraid that I had understood her angry words. After a brief pause, Ricky interjected. "She wants another CAT scan."

"But you had a normal CAT scan six weeks ago. I don't see a justifiable reason to order an unnecessary study." I faked a smile. "Let's do some other tests and go in another direction."

Enid stood, grabbed Ricky's hand, and walked to the door. For the first time, she looked me straight in the eye with her piercing brown eyes. Tears rolled down her face. In broken English she said, "They told me you could help."

She opened the door and walked down the hall, towing Ricky behind.

I hesitated as I watched them leave. I reminded myself that in a funny way, I was helping her. I wasn't wasting her hard-earned money on frivolous tests.

They walked to the front of the office and I headed to see another patient. Out of the corner of my eye, I noticed her paying the bill at the front desk. She emptied a plastic bag, counting out dimes and pennies.

It was then I realized how much this visit had cost Enid. She reminded me of the sick woman who had *suffered much at the hands of many doctors* before she came to Jesus.

Enid's last surgeon had done too much; her new one had done too little. The thought crossed my mind to give Enid her money back. No harm, no foul. I walked towards the front desk. My feet were heavy, my mind confused, wondering the right course of action. She came for reassurance but was leaving no better than when she came.

When I arrived at the front desk, I could see Enid's conflicting emotions, frustration and disappointment mixed with anger and determination. She counted pennies from her purse and realized she had come up short. She couldn't pay all her bill. Embarrassed, she looked at the receptionist and then at me.

I wondered how long it would take her to save up enough pennies to see another doctor. Or would another doctor even take the time to see her? Then I thought about how many bags of change a CAT scan would cost. I looked at her son.

"Ricky, tell your mother I will order her CAT scan. We'll find a way to get it done." I turned, shrugged my shoulders, and sighed to my nurse. "Heck, they do unnecessary tests every day in the emergency room. When you stub your toe, they scan your belly in the ER."

When Enid understood my words, she jumped in the air like a basketball player going for a slam dunk. Her five-foot-two frame almost hit the ceiling. "Gracias. Gracias." She rambled in Spanish so rapidly, I couldn't keep up. I didn't know what she said, but I knew what she meant.

The Surprise

Enid's CAT scan, which was normal six weeks earlier, now showed some abnormalities. A group of enlarging lymph nodes were found in the location of her symptoms. The biopsies showed Hodgkin's Lymphoma. The next step was chemotherapy.

Ricky went with Enid to all her appointments and translated while Enid counted pennies. But it worked.

After finishing treatment, Enid now lives free of pain and cancer. She comes to my office weekly and pays her bill—with loose change.

Lessons Learned

A day worker taught this hardened surgeon some lessons. I was no better than the surgeon before me. I only had the advantage of time, of ordering the right test at the right moment. Sometimes, I wonder what would have happened to Enid had I failed to listen to her request.

The Right Understanding of God

Often, when faced with adversity, we think God doesn't care. We see Him as a disinterested, preoccupied surgeon, ready to move on to the next case. But the reverse is true. God has both the ability and the desire to rescue us in our time of need. He wants His children to experience His power, faithfulness, and goodness. When we ask for bread, our Heavenly Father will not give us a stone. He is not unwilling, reluctant, or annoyed by our asking. He never slumbers. He will freely give us all things through His grace when we ask and believe.

God's understanding of us and of our circumstances penetrates deeper than any CAT scan. Our Heavenly Father has the advantage of time, seeing far beyond a series of doctors trying to piece together a perplexing history. He sees our life—past, present and future—and plans to use them for our good and His purposes.

Hurry Up, God

Often, in times of adversity, we feel like we are dangling off the cliff, holding onto the end of our rope, losing our grip. As our will to hang on weakens, we wonder why God waits. Why do we have to live with such uncertainty?

But we must remember the hinges of Heaven's door have not rusted, so we need to keep knocking. Waiting on God brings perseverance. In the process, we come to the end of ourselves, understanding our frailty, knowing how powerless we are to change things, and how much we need Him.

Our Heavenly Father wants to use life experiences to mature us. As we grow in faith, we learn to abide in His presence. We discover His sufficiency with or without answers. When our world falls apart, we come to understand that His hand is upon us.

Persistence to Seek an Answer

Enid's pain told her to keep pushing, and her persistence paid off. Enid's diligence to find an answer saved her life and changed her destiny. Like Enid, we need a God-driven persistence, fueled by a holy discontent with the way things are. For some of us, deep inside, the Spirit reminds us, things are not okay.

How about you? Do you have an ache in your soul?

How persistent are we in seeking God for our answer? He has promised to provide them if we seek, ask, and knock.

Are we ready to receive the outcome, by laying down our preconceived notions about how and when the answer comes?

When Jesus finished teaching His disciples how to pray, He told them about a man who knocked on his neighbor's door at the midnight hour. The man needed bread. A friend had arrived suddenly and without warning. He shamelessly knocked on his neighbor's door, asking him for help. The neighbor reluctantly gave his friend the bread he needed. Jesus then reminded His disciples of God's desire to grant our requests.

God is more than a fair-weather friend. He is our Heavenly Father who provides what we need.

Persistence Includes Specificity

Enid came into my office with more than a sack of pennies. She knew what she needed—a CAT scan. She asked with specificity.

What are your needs? Do you have a wayward, rebellious child? A chronic health condition? An unexpected financial burden? A frayed relationship? Do you need another chance after failing?

We must learn to be precise. To take some time, filter our thoughts and reflect upon our circumstances. A shotgun prayer that covers all the bases often misses the target. We must learn to focus our request, like a marksman aiming his rifle at the bullseye. We can't pray with persistence until we have narrowed our target.

When we're having trouble being specific, we can ask God to assist. Our Heavenly Father will be more than happy to show us exactly what we need and how we are asking amiss. He wants to show us how to ask according to of His will.

"So I say to you: Ask and it will be given to you; seek and you will find; knock and the door will be opened to you. For everyone who asks receives; he who seeks finds; and to him who knocks, the door will be opened." [81]

*To be a Christian without prayer
is no more possible
than to be alive
without breathing.*

—Martin Luther

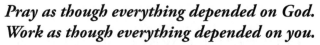

Pray as though everything depended on God.
Work as though everything depended on you.

—Saint Augustine

Chapter 43

THE EMPTY WAITING ROOM

Courage to Overcome Loneliness

I f you are in Christ, you are never alone.

Margie smiled, fidgeted with the tube hanging out her nose, and wore her best poker face. The nurse checked the name on her bracelet and confirmed her identity. Margie gave the nurse one of those condescending looks, the kind she had used for years on her students. "Yep, sweetheart, that's my name. Margie Cook."

I looked at Margie. Even sick, she displayed that *all together* appearance. Her hospital gown looked starched. Not a hair on her head was out of place. But I realized, by her gestures, something other than her name could have been stamped on her identification bracelet: the word *lonely*.

The nurses were finishing up their paperwork before wheeling her into the operating room. They seemed to have no concept of time.

Instead of growing impatient, I stopped and chatted with Miss Margie. "Is there anyone you want me to talk to about your surgery?"

"No, sir." Margie laughed. "I taught junior high math for thirty years. Now, I'm a lot like those math books."

I returned a puzzled look. "What do you mean?"

"I have too many problems."

Taken aback by her honest but humorous insight into her situation, I stood by her bedside, waiting for nurses to finish checking their boxes.

Margie's forehead wrinkled. "I lost my husband six months ago to leukemia, after forty-nine years of marriage. Then I had a heart attack. They put a stent in for the blockage." She pointed to all the bruises on her forearms. "These dern blood thinners are making me bruise everywhere."

I redirected the conversation and asked Margie a question. "Who can I talk to after the surgery?"

"One of my sons will not talk to me. He says I'm always badgering him about his alternative lifestyle. He thinks I need to get with the times and mind my own business." Margie turned her gaze to the wall. "My oldest is a successful broker in New York. He manages billions of dollars in some hedge fund. No need in bothering him. He never calls back anyway."

She rumpled a tissue between her fingers. "I guess you can try his number. You may be able to reach his assistant."

Her restless chatter stopped for a moment. "Don't expect anyone in the waiting room. All my friends in my Sunday School class are in the nursing home now."

Her voice trembled as she pointed to the tube taped to her nose. "Can you pull this water hose out if you don't find cancer?"

I hesitated. "We'll see, Miss Margie."

She scowled at me, making me feel like a third-grader caught red-handed. "You didn't answer my question."

While I tiptoed around the subject, trying to explain the rationale for the tube, the operating crew came, released the bed and pushed her down the hallway.

The nurses thrust open the double doors, wheeling her towards the operating room. Her voice resonated down the hall. "Don't forget. Take out this tube, if you can."

Two hours later, we parked Margie in the recovery room. The operating crew passed off information to the recovery room nurses, checked vital signs and clicked buttons on their computers. I walked through the recovery room doors and entered the waiting room, searching for any family or friends.

I prepared my presentation in my mind. *"First, the good news: Margie's operation was successful. We had bypassed the blockage in her intestines, and her heart had pulled through the surgery. The bad news? The cancer has spread to several places, which were not seen on her CAT scan. It's metastatic cancer. I couldn't get it all."*

I peered into the waiting room where a few people gathered, comforting each other with their presence. Several saw me and jumped up, hoping to hear something about their loved one. One by one, they realized I was not the surgeon they were expecting.

My voice echoed through the waiting room lounge. "Cook family." No one responded. I walked down the hallway, looking for a friend or family member. Another person leaned on the wall, tapping on his cell phone.

"The Cook family?" I queried. The man looked up from his trance, shook his head and quickly tuned back into his cell phone.

No one had shown up for Margie's surgery. At that moment, I remembered the math teacher's words, "Don't expect anyone."

I walked to her bed and checked on her vitals before leaving. Margie woke from her surgery and felt the tube dangling from her nose. "What about the tube?"

I patted her on the shoulder, assuring her everything had gone well. "Nope. The tube can't come out yet."

Margie's consciousness cleared. "Was there anyone in the waiting room?"

My silence answered her question.

She sighed. "I'm not alone, Doctor. The Lord is here with me."

I walked back to my office, wondering how someone so intelligent, generous, and full of spunk had no one there for her in her time of need. Margie had invested her life helping others but had little to show for it. Her sons had abandoned her. Her husband had died. Her friends were too old and feeble to help. According to my calculations, things didn't add up for Miss Margie.

Do the Math

The retired math teacher learned an important life lesson: two and two does not always equal four. In losing all she had—her health, family and friends—she discovered God was all she needed. The math works for us, too.

With God in our equation, typical mathematical rules don't apply. God is anything but typical. With Him, even in difficulty, our blessings multiply. One plus one—Christ and I—equals one hundred, and blessings many times more.

"What, then, shall we say in response to these things? If God is for us, who can be against us. He who did not spare his own Son, but gave him up for us all—how will he not also, along with him, graciously give us all things?" [82]

The unfolding of our friendship with the Father will be a never-ending revelation stretching on into eternity.

—Catherine Marshall

Chapter 44

THE SLEEVE SISTERS

Courage to Change Together

I didn't expect this twist in Sherry's postoperative course.

Sherry had tried for years to lose weight. The Paleo diet. Weight Watchers. Low-fat. Low-carb. You name it, Sherry had tried it.

I remember the day she came into the office to schedule her weight loss surgery. For a year, she had jumped through all the hoops required by her insurance. Now, her day had come.

Her sister Terry came with her and sat beside the exam table. Both suffered with morbid obesity. Both had health conditions hindering weight loss through traditional means. I began Sherry's interview with a question.

"Are you sure you want to go through this? A gastric sleeve can be a high-risk procedure."

Before Sherry could answer, her sister Terry interrupted. "Doctor, we've made a decision. We want to have the surgery together."

I did a double take and looked at Terry. I knew she had more medical problems than her sister. Terry's weight had caused the typical conditions: arthritis, sleep apnea, fatty liver and diabetes. But what sparked Terry's change of heart was her new heart condition.

She said. "The cardiologist told me, surgery was my only hope."

The danger of undertaking this kind of surgery with an arrhythmia raced through my mind. "Terry, the presence of a heart arrhythmia triples your risk of complications. Why do you want to do this?"

A tear slid down Terry's cheek as she looked at Sherry. "If I don't do this and do it soon, I will die."

Sherry butted in. "We want to do this together. We both know about the lifestyle changes we have to make." Sherry paused for a moment. "I will not have the surgery unless you do Terry's."

I felt dismayed at what they were saying. But they had me cornered. I felt like a kid on the playground, with the big bully twisting my arm, making me do something terrible. "Now, wait a minute," I said.

Terry piped in again. "I need her to do this with me. We can hold each other accountable and encourage each other when we are down."

I looked over at Sherry. Her face expressed determination. "I will not have the surgery unless you operate on Terry. It's all or none."

Then they followed with the knock-out punch. "We want our sleeves done on the same day."

I shook my head in disbelief. "Hold on. Are you trying to force me to do this?"

They looked at each other, grinned, and then squinted their eyes at me. In unison, they nodded their heads up and down. "Yes, we are."

I made eye contact with one and then the other. "This is not a two-for-one special. We'll do Sherry's gastric sleeve next Friday, and Terry, we will schedule you for a couple of weeks out."

The room silenced again. By the look on their faces, I could tell they were not budging. Neither said a word. An eternity seemed to pass before Terry finally spoke up. "Same day or nothing."

Sherry put her arm around her sister. "I've already told you. We are doing this together."

After some more counseling and planning, I conceded.

Same-Day Surgery

Sherry and Terry did undergo the operation on the same day. From the recovery room to the floor, they went through the process together. They shared the same hospital room. They walked down the halls of the hospital together. Both were discharged home on the same day. They ate the same diet and started exercising in tandem.

When they returned to the office, I observed results I had not seen in other patients undergoing the same type of surgery. They progressed faster than expected. No whining. No pain. And no complications.

Over the next six months, I watched the sleeve sisters make difficult lifestyle changes—together. When one was down, the other was up. With each step forward, they overcame their challenges. There were there for each other when tempted to eat from boredom, fatigue or depression. They learned about wise food choices and inspired each other.

I noticed an unexplainable synergy between the women. Together, they were far more successful than they ever could have been alone. Their partnership propelled them forward, accelerating their progress. Sherry and Terry were right. Their choice to have surgery and to do life together made a big difference.

The Power of Together

Most of us know what needs to be done to change. Our spirit is willing, but our flesh is weak. We lack the courage and endurance to make progress on our own. In those times, God often shows up—with skin on—in the form of people.

Like oil in a car engine, comforting friends lubricate our rusty parts. We move forward smoother, faster, and with less resistance when we have support. Let's ask ourselves, what changes in life are we considering? What challenges are we facing? Wise people start by building their team.

When we find others who have been through or are going through what we are facing, we benefit one another. We can hold one another accountable. We can share our stories. We can laugh and cry—together. In this way, we fulfill the command to carry each other's burdens.

Going Farther

Nothing beats the encouragement given by someone who has been there previously or who is experiencing similar circumstances. The refreshing presence of those who not only understand, but have walked in our shoes, strengthens us more than any sermon, book or seminar.

Although I could be Sherry's doctor, cheerleader, and coach, I could not be out on the field with her. I stood on the sidelines. With Terry by her side, in the game with her, Sherry found the strength to battle her enemies.

The Sharpening Process

Heaven uses others to help us achieve our dreams. We need people to sharpen our character, notice our weaknesses and encourage our growth. We find friends who have expertise in all different areas of life. Some confidants can help filter our feelings and understand our emotions. Other individuals help us with diet, exercise and personal discipline. We need the wisdom of spiritual mentors and role models as well as the fellowship of people going through the same life season.

We need to be intentional with others—in both giving and receiving help. When we do, a synergism occurs that doesn't happen when we go through life alone.

"As iron sharpens iron, so one person sharpens another."[83]

The One-Anothers

Think of how God used friendships to strengthen, define and sharpen individuals in the Bible. Jonathan encouraged David. Naomi and Ruth walked through tragic events together. In time, they enjoyed the birth of new hope—a marriage, a baby and a heavenly destiny.

Ezra and Nehemiah worked together to rebuild and restore Jerusalem. Daniel and his three comrades committed to faithfulness in captivity. God brought Elisha into Elijah's life, when he was alone and discouraged. Think about Paul, Barnabus, Silas, Titus, Timothy and Dr. Luke, the beloved physician and historian. They ministered together and walked down many a Roman road—side by side.

Then of course, there is Jesus and His disciples. Not only did those twelve rascals change the world—their relationship with Jesus changed them.

God ordained all kinds of relationships to challenge, comfort and help people to pursue their purpose. What makes us think we should be different? Show me your friends today and I'll show you where you will be tomorrow.

Step into Your Purpose

Togetherness is part of God's plan to help us succeed. We must become vulnerable to receive the encouragement of others. Our adversity is wasted if we don't reach out to others in need. But together, like the Sleeve Sisters, we can go to places never before imagined and see a new purpose in our circumstances.

"Two are better than one, because they have a good return for their labor: If either of them falls down, one can help the other up. But pity anyone who falls and has no one to help them up. Also, if two lie down together, they will keep warm. But how can one keep warm alone? Though one may be overpowered, two can defend themselves. A cord of three strands is not quickly broken." [84]

A real friend is one who walks in when the rest of the world walks out.

—Walter Winchell

If you want to go fast,
travel alone.
If you want to go far,
travel together.

—African Proverb

Turn your scars…into stars.
—Robert Schuller

Chapter 45

SCARRED FOR NOTHING

Courage to Grow through Adversity

She wore a long green shawl and covered herself with layers of black clothing. "Graschikfeeta Kukumalaki."

In a British accent, her husband translated. "In Somali, she's saying, take out my gallbladder."

I smiled back at the husband. "Now, you're speaking my language."

Then I started telling one of my standard, *You can't go to heaven with your gallbladder*, jokes, but the husband interrupted me with another question. I'm glad he did.

Considering their culture and religious background, my joke would have created confusion. "What is your name?" I asked.

She looked toward the wall, made no eye contact and left the talking to her husband.

Her husband interrupted. "Her name in English means Sara."

I looked at Sara's clothes and wondered how she endured the hot Texas heat. But then again, Mogadishu makes one feel like a piece of baloney cooked in an oven.

My mind focused back on her issue. "How long has she had pain?"

Sara nodded her head and without waiting for her husband to translate, spoke in Somali to him. I realized she understood English. Her Muslim culture simply would not allow her to talk directly to a person of the opposite sex.

Her husband interjected. "She has had the pain since she was in Somalia."

I looked at the chart. Her birthdate of record displayed 1-1-1970. I knew many Africans who didn't know the day of their birth; when they relocate to the United States, the government gives them all the same birthday: January the first.

Reluctantly, she lay down on the exam table, exposing a small part of her abdomen. I realized she must really be hurting to bare her body. When I examined her belly, two scars were present: one over her gallbladder and the other towards her belly button. The appearance and the location of the scars looked exactly like the ones in people who have already had gallbladder surgery.

Intrigued, I asked her husband. "Where did she get these scars? It looks like she has already had her gallbladder removed."

Her husband shook his head. "No. She still has a gallbladder. This is a Somali custom. When people have pain, we take a hot piece of metal from the fire and burn where it hurts."

I realized that her scars told me more about her symptoms than all the fancy tests on her chart. She had been having gallbladder symptoms for a long while. I looked closer at the skin over her abdomen. Four circular scars, symmetrically placed around her belly button, made the shape of a cross.

Her husband went into detail about the process. Every time his wife had gallbladder symptoms, they burned her belly. Scars upon scars.

This African custom, which springs from witchcraft and traditions, has no power to heal. Many times, it delays people from getting the appropriate management for their problems. On medical mission trips to Africa, I have seen people lose their extremities, waste precious time, and often lose their lives from witchcraft. Not only are these practices unproductive, they can be dangerous.

Can you imagine enduring pain and suffering that in the end leaves you worse off?

Scarred for What?

Our minds can't fathom why someone would injure themselves, endure useless pain, and suffer something which doesn't make them better. Some of these customs, leave the recipient worse off than when they started. But burning your skin with a hot piece of iron pales in comparison to what many people do to themselves. For nothing.

What about You?

Before we point a finger, we should think about our own habits, lifestyle and attitudes. Are we performing a more socially acceptable form of self-mutilation?

Although unintentional, our way of living may be causing us irreversible damage. The first step to healing—spiritually, emotionally, physically, relationally—begins with our perspective. A correct diagnosis leads to a productive treatment. Once we see our life afflictions through the appropriate set of lenses, healing can begin. If we look at our afflictions the wrong way, we will grow bitter. Our suffering becomes unproductive, meaningless and futile. Our scars have no benefit. Those festering maladies on the inside still cause pain. These attitudes often leave us no better and often worse off than before. Much pain, but no gain.

The Personal Pity Party

If we are not careful, we can abide in the *woe is me* attitude. Healing takes time, patience, and understanding. Everyone grieves at their own pace. Time does not heal every wound.

But through God's grace and strength, we don't have to mourn forever. God gives us hope, because we know we are not alone. The greatest comfort in our sorrow springs from knowing that we are in good company. Jesus knows what we are going through, because He has been there. He suffered horrific pain, unfair treatment, and isolation, but in the end, He rose victorious. His resurrection gives purpose to our suffering.

Grin and Bear It

Sometimes we try to endure the pain. We think we are tough enough to get through it on our own. Our *suck it up* attitude often denies the fact that we are wounded. Instead of being honest with ourselves about our needs, we try to cover up our feelings. As a result, we never heal.

We know this truth from medicine. Wounds don't heal when they are covered up. They fester. Wounds need to heal from the inside-out. We must care for them with dressings, ointments and debridement. If skin covers the wound, before it heals on the inside, fluid accumulates. In time, the process becomes an abscess, creating more pain and suffering down the road.

Jesus is our wound care specialist. He bore our pain on the cross. Because He endured suffering for us, we have a friend who can and will carry our burdens. We don't have to neglect or deny our pain. We can face it and place it on His shoulders. He endured horrific afflictions to heal what ails us.

"He was despised and rejected by mankind, a man of suffering, and familiar with pain…and by His wounds we are healed." [85]

Trying to escape our pain is another response. We run as far away from negative experiences as possible. We numb our ache with activities, material things, and short-lived pleasures. But by avoiding our wounds, we never heal completely. We fail to grow through our trials.

The cross reminds us how pain can benefit. We grow emotionally, mentally, and spiritually by bearing hardship.

Bitter or Better

Grief and sorrow can be transformed because of Christ's suffering, death and resurrection. He is with us, today. His joy comes in the morning, if we receive it.

We don't have to bear our burdens alone, Jesus is willing and able to carry them for us. When we try to do things on our own, we are like the Somali woman. We burn ourselves for no reason, adding injury upon injury. Our self-imposed scars bring no benefit. Instead of becoming better, we become bitter, filled with anger and resentment instead of joy, peace, and hope.

Look for the Cross

Without the cross, our suffering doesn't make sense. We never heal. The Somali woman did not perceive that her real solution had been burned onto her belly, in the symbol of the cross.

What about us? Can we see the cross in our suffering? If we look for it, we will find it. Our help is there, waiting for us to recognize it.

Put on the lenses of faith and embrace the power of the finished work of Christ. In so doing, your suffering will begin to make sense. Invite God into your pain. Release control and let Him do what you cannot do for yourself.

Scars Are Good

For God's children, tragedies are never wasted. Our painful experiences are redeemed into something beautiful. We experience the fellowship of His sufferings. Life's sorrows have purpose and meaning. We understand that our afflictions are transient. They are light and momentary. In a little while, we will rejoice over our scars, instead of despising them.

Although we can never fully understand the meaning of suffering in this life, knowing the power of Christ's resurrection gives us hope. The scars, still present on Jesus' resurrected body, are celebrated in heaven. The angels worship, amazed at how God can transform the horrific into something wonderful. Jesus' suffering, while on earth misunderstood, makes sense in eternity. Likewise, if we are in Christ, then someday, our trials will be turned into triumph.

We find what we look for. Do we look for the cross in our affliction? Like Sara, the answer is right in front of us.

"Therefore we do not lose heart. Though outwardly we are wasting away, yet inwardly we are being renewed day by day. For our light and momentary troubles are achieving for us an eternal glory that far outweighs them all." [86]

*Scars are tattoos
with better stories.*

ABOUT THE AUTHOR

 Dr. Chuck Page is the best guy to see on the worst day of your life. A surgeon, storyteller, and coffee addict, Chuck has authored several books for adults and children. Surrendered Sleep: A Biblical Perspective, approaches insomnia from a Christian world view. His children's books Azi's Dance and The One-Eyed Monster Under My Bed are fun stories that show children how God is greater than their fears.

He and his wife Joanna live in Texas with their five children. Chuck enjoys bush-hogging on his tractor, playing with the kids in their triple-decker treehouse, and watching sunsets on the back porch of their farmhouse.

Find inspiring stories, free e-books, podcasts, and devotions at www.charleswpage.com.

ENDNOTES

1   2 Cor. 4:16-18, NIV.

2   Matt. 11:28, NAS.

3   Heb. 4:7, NIV.

4   Is. 55:8-9, NIV.

5   John 5:6, NIV.

6   John 5:8, NIV.

7   John 14:27, NIV.

8   Is. 26:3, NIV.

9   Matt. 8:1-3, NIV.

10   Matt. 8:2-3, NIV.

11   Heb. 4:16, HCSB.

12   Ps. 139:23-24, NIV.

13   Phil. 1:22-24, NIV.

14   Phil. 1:21, NIV.

15   James 1:5, NIV.

16   2 Cor. 5:6-7, NAS.

17   1 Cor. 15:55, NIV.

18   Jn. 15:13-15, NIV.

19   Ps. 139:13-14, NIV.

20   1 Pet. 4:12, ESV.

21   Gal. 5:22-23

22   Phil. 2:17

23   Phil. 2:17, NIV.

24   1 Cor. 5:21, NAS.

25   Phil. 4:6-7, NIV.

26   Is. 41:10, NIV.

27   Psalm 27:1, NKJV.

28   Is. 41:13, NIV.

29   Heb. 13:5-6, NKJV.

30   Rom. 8:15, KJV.

31   Matt. 10:28, NKJV.

32   Is. 41:10, NIV.

33   Deut. 31:6, NKJV.

34   Ps. 34:4, NIV.

35 Gal. 6:9-10, NIV.

36 Jn. 10:4, NIV.

37 Is. 30:21, NIV.

38 Gal. 5:1, NIV.

39 Matt. 18:21-35.

40 Matt. 18:34-35, NKJV.

41 Acts 1:1, NIV.

42 Rom. 5:8, NAS.

43 1 Cor. 2:4-5, NIV.

44 Heb. 10:35-36, NIV.

45 2 Tim. 1:7, NIV

46 Heb. 4:14-16;
    Heb. 10:19-25.

47 Prov. 17:22, NIV.

48 Deut. 31:6, NIV.

49 Heb. 13:5, NAS.

50 Phil. 20:3-4, NIV.

51 James. 5:16, NIV.

52 1 Kings 17:7-24

53 2 Cor. 9:8, NIV.

54 George Matheson.Streams
    in the Desert.L..B. Cowman
    and James Reimann. p. 409..
    Zondervan. 1997.

55 1 Thess. 5:18, NIV.

56 Rom. 12:17-18, NIV.

57 45 James 1:2-3, NIV.

58 Ps. 23:4, NAS.

59 Rom. 8:38-39, NIV.

60 2 Cor. 4:8-11

61 John 10:10, NIV.

62 Phil. 1:21, NIV.

63 Phil. 1:23-24, NAS.

64 Phil. 1:20-24, NIV.

65 Psa. 103:2-3, NIV.

66 Heb. 11:1, NIV.

67 Job 40:7-41:34

68 1 Thess. 5:24, ESV.

69 Job 42:5, NIV.

70 Is. 41:10, NIV.

71 Heb. 6:19, NIV.

72 Jer. 17:14, NIV.

73 Ps. 55:22, NIV.

74 Ps. 34:17, NIV.

75 Rom. 8:37, NIV.

76 Job 10:12, NIV.

77 2 Cor. 1:6, NIV.

78 Eph. 3:16

79 2 Cor. 1:3-4, NIV.

80 2 Cor 1:8, NIV.

81 Luke 11:9-10, NIV

82 Rom. 8:31-32, NIV.

83 Prov. 27:17, NIV.

84 Eccl. 4:10-12, NIV.

85 Is. 53:3-5, NIV.

86 2 Cor. 4:16-17, NIV.

CPSIA information can be obtained
at www.ICGtesting.com
Printed in the USA
BVHW07075710O619
550583BV00001B/12/P